For Students/ Parents/ Teachers

CAREER TRIANGLE

Making Career Clarity Blueprint in 3 Easy Steps

Conquer the Careerdom with Wisdom

MAALI

INDIA • SINGAPORE • MALAYSIA

ISBN
Paperback 979-8-89556-047-1
Hardcase 979-8-89699-326-1

Dedication

I dedicate this book to my father, late ***M.A. Rahaman***, who believed in me and encouraged me to pursue my passion, despite many failures. He taught me how to take responsibility and serve people. Even after two decades of his passing, his guidance, ethics, and honesty are guiding forces in my life.

And to my **mother, Shahzadi Rahaman**, who sacrificed and strived her life for my wellbeing and success in all my endeavors.

CONTENTS

ACKNOWLEDGMENT

Writing this book has been a challenging journey. I spent many sleepless nights and had to sacrifice time with my family and children. The thoughts, ideas, and discussions about careers that I have stored in my mind for years have finally taken shape in this book, which I hope will help students struggling to gain clarity regarding their careers.

I want to honor my paternal grandfather, who instilled in me a sense of discipline, and my maternal grandmother, who taught me the importance of compassion, sacrifice, and leading a simple life. I am deeply grateful to my father, who instilled in me a sense of responsibility and a commitment to service. He taught me the transformative power of education, a value I carry with me to this day. My mother supported me in every aspect of my life, granting me the freedom to think and act independently. I am fortunate to have inherited their values.

This book would not have become a reality without the unwavering support of my wife, Syeda Asia Sultana. She believed in my potential and motivated me to share my knowledge and experience on careers with society. I am also grateful to my children, Shaya and Asad, who sacrificed their time with me and patiently waited to see me become an author.

To my brothers, Dr. Dowlath, Rafiq, and Humayun, thank you for encouraging me to write this book and for the many discussions that contributed to this content.

I am grateful to my former boss and mentor, Sri Shaik Mohammad Iqbal, IPS, Inspector General of Police (Rtd), whose sincerity and dedication to service have inspired me and shown me that success and satisfaction come from serving others.

My heartfelt thanks to my dearest friends, Yadati Subramanyam, Sunku Srinivas, and Syed Ashwaque Hussain, who have supported and motivated me throughout my life. Our many discussions provided invaluable content for this book, drawn from real-life experiences.

Finally, I want to thank the Almighty for granting me the knowledge and wisdom to complete this book.

Last but not least, I would like to express my gratitude to everyone who has supported me, directly or indirectly, in this project.

PREFACE

A career represents one's entire life. If the career is taken care of adequately, life will be peaceful and prosperous. At the end of the day, everybody, whether he is the CEO of a company or an employee, wants to be happy and healthy; otherwise, life will be frustrating and futile. However, individuals tend to neglect career planning as they live in this society. Every year, we see tons of graduates with unfit, misfit, and misguided careers, creating more structural unemployment. Many students are becoming victims of the whims and fancies of their parents, relatives, peers, and other stakeholders, struggling to withstand life for themselves, and are forced to take up careers that they don't enjoy or feel aren't purposeful, thus creating a mess in society.

Academic Education and career education should go hand in hand. Unfortunately, we have poor access to career education. There is a huge gap between one's college and one's career. We have to fill this gap with career education, ensuring a smooth transition from college to a company. The entire burden of choosing the right career sits on the shoulders of students. However, the students have fewer resources to make well-informed decisions about their careers in this era of information overload.

In this context, it is the right time to attempt to create frameworks, processes, and well-sorted information to push every student toward a fitting career and great fortune and to become productive in building our nation.

The students need to awaken and demand career education from their schools and parents. Schools and colleges should develop human resources in career education, create an environment for career counseling, and set them up with dedicated Career Counselors. Instead of putting pressure on the students, the parents should provide them with access to career counseling and allow them to choose the career they love. The teachers should also enhance their counseling skills, provide quality information on careers, and embed it in their teaching wherever necessary.

In the wake of rapid changes in the world of diverse careers, the work in hand is an attempt to provide a framework for students to understand themselves and write their *Career Clarity Blueprint*, which guides them throughout their careers. I have tried to depict three crucial areas to build a fail-proof career in this book. Mastering these three areas will give you a fail-proof and future-fulfilling career. These areas are:

1. Understanding Yourself – Self-Awareness
2. Knowing the various Career Paths/Options.
3. Introducing the World of Work.

These three critical areas decide the entire trajectory of a student's career. Triangle, the strongest form I call in the above three areas, will form a robust construction of your career. Please don't skip any chapter; chapters are sequentially arranged using a step-by-step method and follow the instructions at the end of the book. Everything will be clear, and the '*Career Clarity Blueprint*' will be ready to guide you in your career.

I sincerely feel that this book will not only provide a platform for high school students through their graduation but will also be helpful to parents, teachers, career counselors, and people with a general interest in the subject to get an idea about careers at the macro level and design a framework of their own accordingly.

I have tried my best to make this book the best for students, yet I feel that the readers are the best judges of its merits. Therefore, I invite suggestions to enhance and improve the value of the work.

Career Traingle

Maali

INTRODUCTION

The education of students in their teenage years forms an incubation period for their careers. If they make the right decisions in their teenage years, their careers will lead them to be happy and healthy; otherwise, they will be stuck leading unhappy, unhealthy, unsatisfactory, and unsuccessful lives. They may also have to struggle throughout their life, even for survival, due to unthoughtful decisions taken during their teenage years. Mistakes may happen at any stage, from selecting the right career, stream, or course to college. The mismatch between their education and employment will make their career and lives miserable and futile.

If the student takes care of this in the early stages of their studies, this chaos can be overcome. The student has to understand the entire gamut of careers to position themselves as a successful person both in their career and life. This book explains three essential steps: knowing oneself, knowing various career options, and knowing the occupations available. Mastering these three stages makes a student super successful in their career as well as in life.

I have been exploring the subject for 25 years and have done an in-depth analysis of career planning on how one should decide on their own. My father used to teach me a sense of vision and mission, passion, career planning, leadership, etc., during my graduation. I could not understand what he was saying at that time. When I was 23, he passed away, and I had to take on my family's responsibility, including my three younger brothers, who were then studying in their primary and high schools. It was a huge responsibility since I had just gotten out of college then. However, I tried to explore career planning aspects with my father's ideas and knowledge and tried to master them. I read many books on career planning and struggled a lot in our career journeys. Still, I felt some kind of deficiency in career planning and found several mistakes at that time in selecting the right careers, courses, and colleges for them to position them in the right place. Later, I decided to deep-dive into career planning. I decided to help young students with the right knowledge that I acquired during my journey of career finding. I have mentored and guided many students to select fitting careers and have helped them in achieving their life goals.

Unfortunately, we have a poor sense of career planning and limited access to good-quality career counseling in India. We accept things the way they come to us in our lives. However, understanding the need for career planning in one's teenage years gives them more clarity in a career, which leads them to a happy and healthy life. I believe that the best person to know about himself is himself primarily.

In this book, I have tried to portray the fundamental and essential ingredients of career planning and how to understand them and put them into action for a sustainable career and life. I promise that if the student embeds these essential elements in their mind and implements them in their daily life during their schooling days, success is inevitable. If somewhere they think they are failing in their career, they wouldn't because these elements are well-structured and form the building blocks to build a rock-solid foundation.

Career building is not just selecting the right course, college, or studying in the right country. If this were so, all the students who had studied in a particular course or college or country should have been successful, and all others unsuccessful. But it is not like that. Some students may succeed, some may not, and this is something beyond their success or failure. You have to look beyond just attractive courses, posh colleges, or crazy countries. Many students who don't have minimum facilities will reach that step of success. That means there is something beyond all these things you have to master.

You must have found many books on what to study after 10+2 with information about the courses and colleges, etc., but what these books tend to miss out on are the essential elements for career planning: how to select a right-fitting career based on your personality, interest, and skills, how to come out of dilemmas while choosing a career, course, and college, etc.

After years of research and analyzing the successful and unsuccessful students and adults in their careers, I have tried to unleash the secret of career building and design a step-by-step and holistic approach to guarantee success in your career and life. We can't take back the mistakes we made while planning our careers. Thus, I have designed the career-building in three easy steps that cover the fundamental elements of the career-building, viz.,

1. Know Yourself - Your personality, interest area, life skills, etc.

2. Know how to select a fitting career, course, college options, etc.

3. Know various occupations and their dimensions.

Understanding some concepts, like your calling in life, vision, mission, occupation, etc., may be difficult for you due to their depth. You may seek the help of your parents or a career counselor wherever you feel that something is difficult to understand since these concepts are essential, without which the idea of a career isn't complete. However, you can use this book during your teenage years and throughout your entire career and life. If you miss out or neglect to master any of the elements, your career will be in the doldrums. Again, you have to start right from the beginning, but you will have missed out on a lot of time and opportunities, lagging behind many of your peers.

This book will serve you as a companion or friend throughout your career and life. Whenever you feel stuck, confused, distracted, slowed, stressed, or even like a failure, simply revisit this book and get back on track.

"If you can view the Earth like a bird,
you can see the sky as a man."

AN IDEA OF CAREERS

Students often think that their career planning only starts after their academic education is over. Most students, especially in India, experience great shock once they find it challenging to get into the workforce. Soon after, they realize that they have gotten into an unfit career. Still, they can't undo and redo the entire academic education, and they have to continue with the unfit career throughout their lives, bearing the burden of stress and dissatisfaction. That is what is happening with many of the students. For example, suppose you judge a fish by its ability to climb a tree or a monkey by its ability to swim. In that case, they both fail because each has its own abilities, limitations, and unique capabilities. Every student is outstanding. Each of them is unique, and their ability will be known when they are judged with proper tests.

Many students think that whatever they are planning during their high school years is education planning, and they believe that career planning will start only after completing their formal education. However, they get confused about whether their education will decide their career or whether their career choice will determine their path of education. It is just like the debate over whether the tree came first or the seed. One should start career planning during their high school days because choosing the right stream or subjects in +2 and the right course and college would decide one's entire career trajectory. For them, the students who follow this path manage to get into employment, a profession, or entrepreneurship as if it were a cakewalk.

A career represents one's entire life. We suffix the word career with different words. The combination of career phrases like career planning, Career Building, Career Development, and Career Management represents different meanings applicable to different stages of life, starting from Education to Retirement. These words are used interchangeably in different contexts when talking about careers. Here is an analysis to give students an idea about their career and the stages to indicate different stages of life.

Career Planning	High School to College	Focus on Knowledge
Career Building	After College to the beginning years of the job, say up to five years	Focus on Skills
Career Development	From 5 years to 15 years of experience	Focus on Attitude
Career Management	From 15 years to retirement	Focus on Wisdom

More than 70% of high school students and their parents think that career planning only starts after graduation. They skip the crucial 1st stage and jump to the next step. This mismatch haunts them throughout their careers up to their retirement, leading to frustration, dissatisfaction, and stress, and soon, they begin struggling for growth and development. However, for students who are aware of and follow these above-mentioned stages, admission to the best courses and colleges will be a cakewalk for them. Securing good jobs will ultimately lead to fulfillment of life and great success.

This book touches upon all the stages, mainly focusing on career planning, which mostly occurs in the early stages of high school until graduation, during one's teenage years. Some of the concepts seem highly philosophical and profound; thus, it is difficult to understand some of the concepts in this book at this tender age.

It is essential to seed these concepts in one's mind at this age - embedded and understood with clarity and growing along with one's age and experience throughout their career's journey. The students should try to understand these concepts and keep in mind these essential points.

This book introduces a student to all the aspects and elements one needs to consider while thinking about the idea of a career.

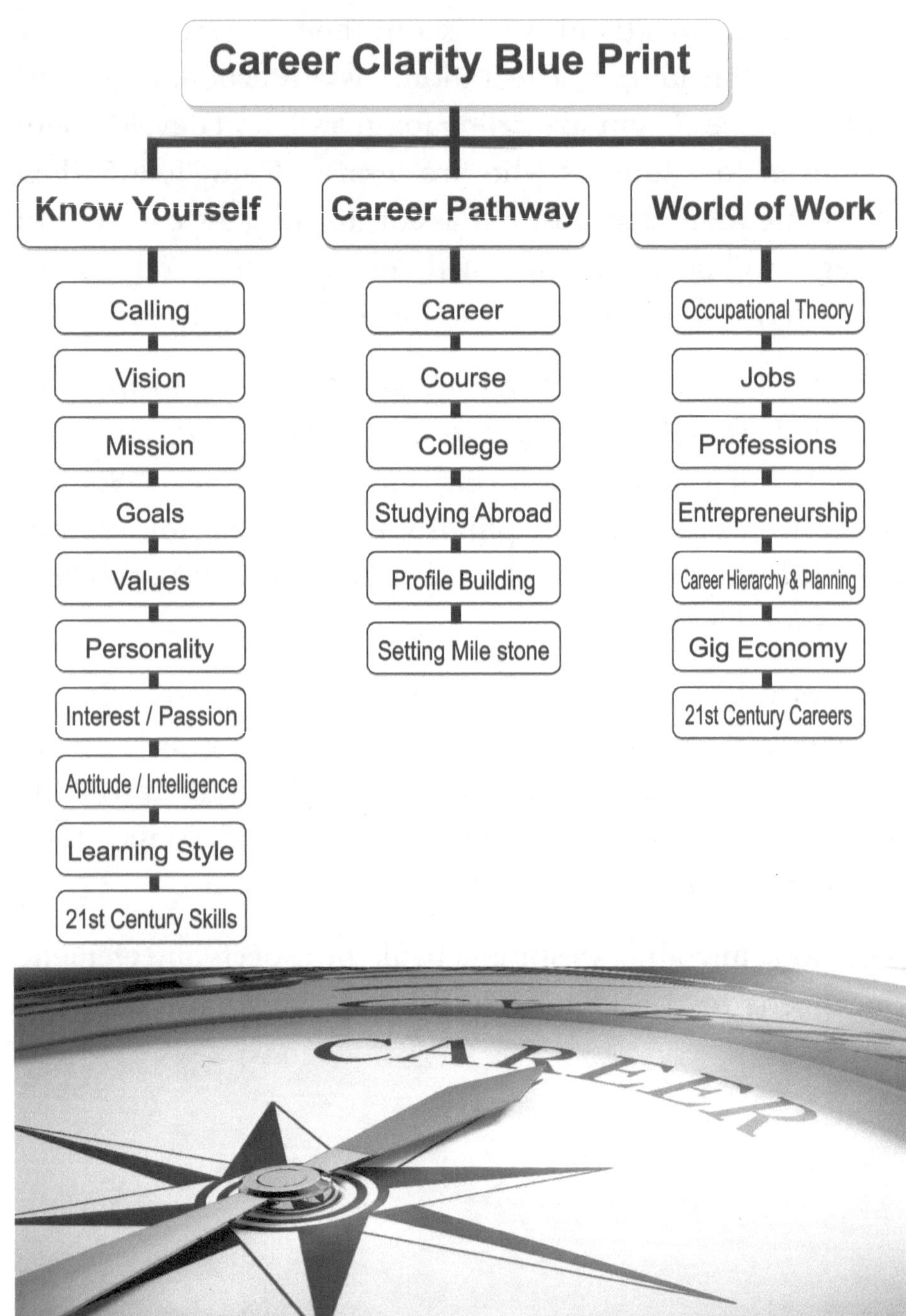
Career Clarity Blue Print
Know Yourself
Calling
Vision
Mission
Goals
Values
Personality
Interest / Passion
Aptitude / Intelligence
Learning Style
21st Century Skills
Career Pathway
Career
Course
College
Studying Abroad
Profile Building
Setting Mile stone
World of Work
Occupational Theory
Jobs
Professions
Entrepreneurship
Career Hierarchy & Planning
Gig Economy
21st Century Careers
CAREER

STEP I: KNOW YOURSELF

How much do you know yourself? You must be wondering about the logic behind posing this question, but the truth is that no one can choose a career path if they do not truly know themselves. What would you do if someone else is trying to form your career? You won't be able to survive because no one truly knows you better than you. Knowing yourself is the fundamental aspect of your career-building. It lays a strong foundation for your career. Unless you know yourself properly, you will not be able to select the right-fit career for yourself. You are the best person to understand yourself and, after that, your parents and teachers. So, take out a pen and paper, write down something about yourself, and analyze what comes to your mind. In this section, the following topics will cover various dimensions of *yourself*.

1. Explore your calling in life, vision, and mission
2. Understand your personality, passion, interest, and values
3. Master life skills
4. Understand your learning style, etc.

Mastering the above dimensions of yourself will help you to identify the career that will be suitable for you. Selecting the right-fit career will eventually give you satisfaction, and you will feel more fulfilled in life.

Chapter 1

CALLING

"To realize one's destiny is a person's only real obligation."

– Paulo Coelho

Now that you have sat with yourself and written about your inner desires and visions, you must have understood the importance of calling. The word 'Calling' doesn't only apply to saints or highly intellectual people; it's an indication that your life is worth something and that you have a purpose in life. Every human being has this calling once in a while. As we grow, we begin to understand our purpose in life, our goals, or our aims that work to define us. Each and every student must understand and adhere to this calling. It is through this path that you can achieve your goal. Once this has been realized, the journey of life will become satisfactory and fruitful.

But what does calling really mean? Each of us is unique in our abilities and passions. We choose our aims based on our skills. After we have drawn a mind map of our career journey, we get this strong impulse to fulfill a purpose. This purpose is what drives us. It pushes us forward to achieve our goals. Our desire to achieve this purpose leads us forward, and only then do we feel fulfilled in life. Whatever occupation, vocation, or trade you wish to choose, keep this calling in mind, and you will never feel drained or without motivation.

Our callings are actually God's voice that directs us toward our purpose in life. At some point, all of us are bound to choose a vocation. No matter where our heart drives us, we must adhere to this calling. It is this calling that makes us who we are and helps us achieve success. If we are meant to succeed in life, we must listen to these callings and watch the building blocks shape the path of our careers.

God has a blueprint for each of us, and we must follow His plan to discover our vocation. If we can find our vocation allotted by God, we will have peace and clarity in life. God speaks through our inner and outer experiences. When we respond to His voice, we will have more clarity when choosing a career.

How to Explore Your Calling in Life:

1. Find what attracts you more. Note down a list of things that seem inviting to you, things you love to do tirelessly without straining yourself, and that is what makes you forget time.

   ____

   ____

   ____

   ____

2. Write down responses to the question, "What is my calling?" below. After completing your responses, you will automatically understand what your calling is in life.

___

___

___

___

3. Ask your parents and trusted elders, "What would be your passion or niche as per their observation?"

___

___

___

___

4. Make a list of your core values and write them down. This list will result in finding your calling.

___

___

___

___

Now that you have understood your calling, the next step is understanding the vision behind your career choice. Visions are meant to direct your way and guide you toward success. Head to the next chapter to understand more about visions.

Chapter 2

VISION

"Without a vision, people perish."

– Proverbs 29:18

Calling and Vision represent the same thing, but vision is a futuristic word. When one hears the word "vision," what comes to mind is a virtual plan we wish to make a reality. In other words, vision paints a picture of the Calling at a specific time in the future.

Let's understand this with an example: If you find your calling and it leads you to become a scientist and serve society, your vision will be to complete your Ph.D. in Sciences and take up scientific research as a career.

Vision is the ability to think about or plan the future with our imagination or wisdom. Vision gives us a clear sense of purpose. It is the mental picture of the future we desire. It is more than just a goal; it is the embodiment of our hopes and dreams in a particular area of expertise. It is a picture of what has not yet happened but what the future may hold. Our passion and goals drive the vision, reflected through the real effort that we make to create tangible results.

Create a vision board by going through a discovery process to clarify what's most important for you.

Why do we need Vision?

"Your vision will become clear only when you can look into your own heart. Who looks outside, dreams; who looks inside, awakes."

– Carl Jung

- Vision gives inspiration and motivation.
- It creates energy and enthusiasm in your efforts.
- It increases commitment toward your set goals.
- It will produce persistence in stressful times.
- It keeps you away from distractions and focused on your aim, reminding you what your dreams are.
- It defines your short- and long-term goals and helps guide your decisions along the way.

How to Set a Vision?

- Evolve the Vision arena from your Callings.
- Explore your passion and talents. You are made with God-given talents. Just feel it.
- Spend time with people you admire and ask them questions about how, where, why, and what they do.
- Imagine what your life will look like in the future.

- Don't limit yourself to dreaming. Your vision should be exciting.
- Take feedback from your family and people you trust, whether your vision is on point or not, and make changes accordingly.
- Seek accountability from dear ones to hold you accountable for staying on course.
- Be flexible and open to any changes in your vision. It is a living thing.

Write down the answers to the following questions. This will become your vision.

1. What type of man or woman do you want to be?

   ____
   ____
   ____
   ____

2. What do you want your family to be?

   ____
   ____
   ____
   ____

3. What would you like your career to be?

   ____
   ____

____

____

4. What would your lifestyle be?

____

____

____

____

Effects of Not Having a Vision

> ***"If you don't know where you are going, you will likely end up somewhere else."***
>
> ***– Yogi Berra***

You must work on setting your vision before anything else. Otherwise, you will lose many things like your dreams, inspiration, enthusiasm, passion, commitment, direction, goals, and flexibility in your career and life. All these things are indispensable for your career and life because they tie together all the essential elements one needs. As the saying goes, 'One shot, many birds.' Hopefully, you won't miss out on such a vital thing in life.

As per the next step, it is important to pay attention to your mission. After you have determined your vision, a mission plan is the next step. Jump to the next chapter to know all about it.

Chapter 3

MISSION STATEMENT

"A personal mission statement becomes the DNA for every other decision we make."

– Stephen R. Covey

You must be wondering why the mission needs to be talked about here. When we think about our purpose in life, we must always have a mission to fulfill. Without a mission, there is no particular course to tread upon. The mission is the next step after forming a vision. The mission statement is a brief explanation of what you want to achieve in your career. You can use it to outline your goals, draw action plans, apply your skillset, and set specific tasks to reach your goals. A mission statement is a set of guidelines that govern how you work toward specific outcomes. It sets the rules for what you aim to do and how you will do it in your career journey.

Benefits of Having a Mission Statement

- Your Mission Statement helps you determine what you are passionate about and understand what motivates you.
- It helps you figure out what you want to do in your career, such as the roles you want to have, advancement

opportunities that suit your goals, and industries you want to work in.

- It improves focus on the areas of your professional and career development.
- It makes decision-making easy and clarifies what you want to achieve.
- It serves as a reminder of your goals and helps you retain focus and build resilience to overcome obstacles as they come along the way.

How to Write a Mission Statement

You should align your mission statement with your values and interests. The following are the main ingredients of a mission statement:

1. **Establish Your Values**

   Start by writing down the values and aspects of your personal and professional life that matter the most to you. Some examples of values are acceptance, adventure, bravery, community, family, friendship, growth, Happiness, hard work, honesty, integrity, kindness, knowledge, patience, peace, popularity, power, quality, respect, responsibility, spirituality, stability, success, time management, wealth, wisdom, etc.

2. **Determine Your Interest**

   Your interest is the primary aspect of your life and career that keeps you passionate about and invested in achieving your goals. List hobbies, activities, social causes, and other elements that interest you. Each interest should relate to your core values.

3. **Identify Your Strengths**

   Make a list of tasks you excel in and the skills you have developed to identify the actionable elements of your background that will help you reach your goal.

4. **Describe Your Goals**

   Goals help you make progress by creating measurable growth achievements. Your values, interests, and strengths identify the central goal you want to achieve.

5. **Draw an Action Plan**

   Relate your skill directly to your goals by writing specific, actionable steps you plan to take to reach your goals. These steps will give you an overview of what you should do to form goals that align with your values and interests.

6. **Revisit Your Statement Often**

   Your mission statement is like a guide to you. You should revisit it frequently to make sure it still aligns with your goals, and your actions align with your mission statement. Place it somewhere you can see it every day, such as on your desk. If your career path changes or another element of your life shifts, review and revise your mission statement to fit your new values, skills, and goals.

Answer the following questions, and it will become your mission statement:

1. What is most important to you?

____

2. What legacy do you want to leave for the world, and how do your skills allow you to do that?

3. Ask your parents and peers what they consider to be your greatest strength.

4. What are your biggest goals in life?

5. What are your values?

____

____

____

____

Since you have now determined what your mission is, it is now time to set your goals. You need to draw a plan according to which your journey will be. When thinking about your goals, think long and hard. With this in mind, switch to the next topic to understand more about forming your goals.

Chapter 4

GOALS

"A goal without a plan is only a dream."

– Brian Tracy

Has anyone ever questioned you about your goal in life? Did you stand confused when asked such an important question? What are your goals, and why should you have them? Goals evolve from your vision and mission statement. A goal is an idea of the future or desired result you envision, plan, and commit to achieving. Before you start envisioning your goals, write down whatever you wish to achieve in your life or in a particular timeline. You must remember that you must try to reach your goals within a finite time by setting deadlines. This will not only help you stay on track but will also keep you efficient.

Goals help you make progress by creating measurable growth achievements. You have to identify your main goal using your values, interests, and strengths in order to achieve them. You have to set specific, quantifiable goals that provide a path to improve your career. This way, you will have a planned route toward a successful career.

- Goal setting gives you a **framework** to achieve certain milestones in your life.

- Goal setting **provides** a path for you to execute them.

There are two types of goals: 1. Short-term goals 2. Long-term goals.

1. **Short-term Goals:** These are the more immediate goals you form to achieve your long-term goals. Short-term goals are what create your path and bring you one step closer to your larger goals. These goals are meant to make your work easier and help you to relieve your burdens. Short-term goals are meant to be achieved somewhere around the timeline of a year or less. E.g., you can set a goal to achieve an 'A' Grade in your academics in that year, or you may plan to crack some entrance exams within a year.

2. **Long-term Goals:** These goals are the bigger goals you want to achieve over several years, say 5 to 10 years. Several short-term goals and milestones together may form your larger goals. For example, you can set a target of securing a seat in a reputed university in a particular country or getting your dream job or desired profession.

There are three types of goals, namely, personal, professional, and financial goals, that are important building blocks for your career.

1. **Personal Goals:** These goals are set for your personal life and help you gain personal achievement. These goals may be for advancing in your hobbies, health, or education. With these personal goals, you can

achieve success in your career. You can also include achievements made in these goals on your resume while applying for jobs.

2. **Professional Goals:** These goals are set for your professional life and help you gain professional achievement. These goals help you get into a professional course like completing your M.B.A., Engineering, Medical degree, Law, etc., and entering into a related career within a particular time frame.

3. **Financial Goals:** These goals help achieve your individual intended financial status to lead your dream Lifestyle in life. Though you need not hurry to achieve your financial goals, you must keep in mind that they are part of the Complete Career Plan.

How to Set Goals

You can set your goals in different ways. However, your goals should have five key elements that are SMART and achievable. These five elements form the 'SMART' goals framework. The SMART framework is as follows:

1. **Smart:** Your Goal should be clear and well-defined. Generalized goals will not give you an accurate direction. E.g., In place of 'I have to perform well in final exams,' you can set it as 'I have to get A+ Grade or 10 GPA in the final exams.'

2. **Measurable:** Your Goal should be measurable in terms of numbers, amounts, dates, etc., and you must set

milestones to achieve those goals. E.g., If you are all set to reach a 10 GPA in your final exams, you have to get 95% in your internal exams.

3. **Achievable:** Your Goal should be achievable or attainable; otherwise, you will end up demoralizing yourself and lose self-confidence. E.g., If you are not doing well in the internal exams and are unable to top your college, it will end up discouraging you, and this will shake your self-confidence for your future endeavors.
4. **Relevant:** Your Goal should be relevant to the direction you want to achieve your long-term goal in. For example, achieving a 10 GPA in your finals will help you secure a seat in your dream college and course.
5. **Time-bound:** Your Goal should be Time-bound. When you set a deadline for your goal, it will give you a sense of urgency, and you will be able to achieve it quickly.

Your goals should be of primary importance to you and should motivate you immensely; they should give you considerable value in achieving them. They should be written properly and followed through with an Action Plan. Write down your goals in the following table.

Goal	Short Term	Long Term
Personal		
Professional		
Financial		

If You Don't Have Goals:

- You will get distracted from your mission and vision.
- You will be directionless in your career and life.
- You will curtail your likelihood of success.
- Your values will go to waste and be futile.

As your goals will slowly form the shape of your career, you will also come across an important factor that will drive you to success. This factor occurs in the form of values. Whatever you wish to achieve, you will often find yourself at a crossroads where your values will play a great role. During this crucial time, you will have to make use of your values and choose the right path for yourself to achieve success. Dive into the next chapter to learn more about the importance of values.

Chapter 5

VALUES

"Open your arms to change, but don't let go of your values."

– Dalai Lama

As kids, we are taught the importance of adhering to our parents' or society's principles and values. We watch the people in our surroundings follow these values, and that is how we understand how important these values are for us to live our lives. Values are the fundamental beliefs of a person. They are the guiding principles to help you understand the difference between right and wrong. Values are the standards we set that help us form judgments about what is essential in life. There are three types of core values that we must keep in mind:

1. **Personal Values**: These are the things necessary for you. The characteristics and behavior that motivate you and guide your decisions. E.g., health, happiness, lifestyle, popularity, appearance, family life, etc.,

2. **Character Values:** These are the universal qualities required to exist as a good human being. These values help in your career and jobs. E.g., honesty, loyalty,

commitment, dependability, efficiency, reliability, consistency, etc.,

3. **Work Values:** These values help you find what you need in a career and give you complacency and satisfaction. These also allow you to grow professionally. E.g., Work ethics, responsibility, professionalism, security, honesty, and integrity, dependability, adaptability, self-motivation, positive attitude, etc.,

Importance of Values In Career and Life:

Your values are important because they help you to grow and develop into a wonderful human being. They allow you to create the future you want to see. Values help you to:

- Find your purpose
- Face difficult situations
- Make sound decisions
- Clear out the clutter
- Choose the right career
- Develop a sense of self-awareness
- Increase your confidence
- Increase the overall happiness level

Write down your values below and keep them in mind. Practice them in your day-to-day situations and master them.

Personal Values

____

____

____

____

Character Values

____

____

____

____

Work Values

____

____

____

____

Chapter 6

PERSONALITY

"It is up to each person to recognize his or her true preferences."

– Isabel Briggs Myers

Individual personalities vary from person to person, and the 'one size fits all' approach is not applicable in this regard; rather, it is strongly discouraged. Personality plays a vital role in career exploration, serving as a cornerstone of one's overall career and life. Understanding your personality well is important for choosing a career that suits you. Opting for a career that aligns with your personality would bring you success, satisfaction, health, peace of mind, etc. It allows you to focus on your work without any dissatisfaction or frustration.

Personality is the characteristic set of behavior, cognition, and emotional patterns that evolve from biological and environmental factors. It is a relatively stable set of characteristics that influences your behavior, determines how you adjust to your environment, and reacts to specific situations. It denotes your unique way of managing various situations based on your personal understanding.

PERSONALITY TYPES

Isabel Myers and Katherine Myers-Briggs developed the Myers-Briggs Type Indicator (MBTI), a personality type indicator based on Carl Jung's 'theory of psychological types.' The MBTI is a widely used psychometric questionnaire designed to measure psychological preferences in how individuals perceive the world and make decisions.

The MBTI identifies personality preferences in four dimensions or dichotomies. It refers to a system for understanding human behavior based on the belief that there are 16 distinct personality types, and each person has one type that most accurately describes them.

1. Where you focus your attention –

   Extraversion (E) or Introversion (I)

2. The way you take in the information –

   Sensing (S) or Intuition (N)

3. How do you make decisions –

   Thinking (T) or Feeling (F)

4. How do you deal with the world –

   Judging (J) or Perceiving (P)

Let's understand each dimension.

First Criterion:

Extraversion (E) – It signifies the source and direction of a person's energy expression, mainly in the external world.

Introversion (I) – An introvert has a source of energy, mainly in their internal world.

Second Criterion

Sensing (S) – It represents how someone perceives information they receive directly from the external world.

Intuition (N) – It indicates that a person mainly believes in the information they receive from the inner or imaginative world.

Third Criterion:

Thinking (T) – It represents how a person processes information, mainly making decisions based on logic.

Feeling (F) – It means that, as a rule, they make a decision based on emotion, i.e., what they feel they should do.

Fourth Criterion:

Judging (J) – It reflects how a person implements the information they have processed, i.e., organizes all life events and generally sticks to plans.

Perceiving (P) – It indicates that they are inclined to improvise and explore alternative options.

Each individual falls under a four-letter acronym, representing one preference from each criterion. All possible combinations of preferences in the four dimensions yield 16 personality types in each dimension from each criterion, viz.,

ESTJ, ISTJ, ENTJ, INTJ, ESTP, ISTP, ENTP, INTP, ESFJ, ISFJ, ENFJ, INFJ, ESFP, ISFP, ENFP, INFP.

For example:

- ESTJ stands for Extraversion, Sensing, Thinking, and Judging.
- INFP stands for Introversion, Intuition, Feeling, and Perceiving.

FIND YOUR PERSONALITY

Let us find your personality by selecting it from the list.

Where do you focus your attention and express your energy?	**Write Your Preference.**
EXTRAVERSION (E) • you seek interaction with people. • enjoyed while in groups • communicate with others by talking • always outgoing and sociable. • like variety and action orientation • involved with people • learn by doing or discussing • do - think - do • spend your energy • enjoy a wide circle of friends.	

INTROVERSION (I) • you like to be alone • enjoy one-on-one • communicate with others by writing. • always reserved and private. • want to focus on one thing at a time • work with ideas. • learn by reflection and thinking. • think - do - think • Conserve your energy. • enjoy a small circle of friends.	
The way you take in the information	**Write Your Preference.**
SENSING (S): • you focus on what is real and actual • prefer facts and concrete information • Pay attention to details. • observe and remember sequentially. • you are down-to-earth • learn step-by-step • focus on the present • rely on experience.	

• choose things as they are • value practical applications.	
INTUITION (N): • you focus on possibilities • prefer abstract insights. • Focus on the big picture. • see patterns and meaning. • have your head-in-the-clouds • learn by leaping anywhere • Focus on the future. • rely on inspiration and imagination. • like to try new things. • value ingenuity	
How you make decisions	**Write Your Preference.**
THINKING (T): • you prefer to analyze the problem • are objective. • are tough-minded • value justice. • are reasonable and fair. • Use cause-and-effect reasoning • are good at critiquing. • prefer to be direct.	

• usually don't take things personally • can be seen as insensitive.	
FEELING (F): • you prefer to sympathize with the problem • are subjective. • are tender-hearted • value harmony. • are compassionate and accepting • are guided by personal values • are good at complimenting • prefer to be tactful • usually take things personally • can be seen as overemotional	
How you deal with the world.	**Write Your Preference.**
JUDGING (J): • you value structure. • tend to work now & play later • like things settled and decided. • prefer things to be organized • make lists and use them • value punctuality. • prefer to have deadlines. • like to complete projects. • are goal-oriented	

• value order. • like to follow timetables.	
PERCEIVING (P): • you are easy-going • tend to play now & work later. • like to be spontaneous. • prefer things to remain open-ended • make lists and lose them • leave the thing to the last minute. • often ask, "What deadline?" • like to start projects. • are process-oriented • value flexibility. • enjoy last-minute pressures	

Now, write down the four letters representing your four preferences from the four questions - these will determine your personality type. The description for each type is given below.

Let's describe each type. Out of 16 personality types, only one relates to you; the other 15 relate to other types. Check them out.

Type	Description	Characteristics	Famous Personalities
ISTG	Reliant	Quiet, serious, thorough, dependable. Practical, realistic, organized. Values traditions and loyalty.	Henry Ford, George Washington, Narayana Murthy.
ISFJ	Nurturer	Quiet, friendly, responsible, conscientious. Loyal, considerate, creates harmonious environments.	Agatha Christie, Mother Teresa, Sachin Tendulkar
INFJ	Mystic	Seeks meaning and connection. Insightful, committed to values, organized in implementing vision.	Carl Jung, J.K. Rowling, and Narendra Modi
INTJ	Freethinker	Original minds, driven, logical. Organized in pursuing goals, skeptical and independent.	John F. Kennedy, Manmohan Singh, Homi Bhabha.

Type	Description	Characteristics	Famous Personalities
ISTP	Realist	Tolerant, flexible, acts quickly to find solutions. Analytical, values efficiency, interested in cause and effect.	Venus Williams, Isaac Newton, Amartya Sen.
ISFP	Aesthete	Quiet, friendly, sensitive. Enjoys the present, loyal to values. Dislikes conflicts, respects others' opinions.	Lata Mangeshkar, Michael Jackson, Brad Pitt.
INFP	Dreamer	Idealistic, loyal, and curious. Seeks congruence with values, adaptable, and flexible.	William Shakespeare, Rabindranath Tagore, Amit Trivedi.
INTP	Wizard	Logical explanations, theoretical, analytical. Focused problem solvers. Skeptical and critical.	Albert Einstein, Larry Page, Dr. APJ Abdul Kalam.
ESTP	Adventurer	Flexible, pragmatic, and energetic. Focuses on immediate results, learns best through doing.	Donald Trump, Mike Tyson, Dhyan Chand.

Type	Description	Characteristics	Famous Personalities
ESFP	Joker	Outgoing, accepting, exuberant. Brings common sense to work, adaptable, and spontaneous. Learns best by trying new skills.	Katy Perry, Will Smith, Rajesh Khanna.
ENFP	Visionary	Enthusiastic and imaginative. Sees life as full of possibilities. Flexible, relies on improvisation, and verbal fluency.	Ravi Shankar, Shankar Mahadevan, Ellen DeGeneres
ENTP	Innovator	Quick, ingenious, strategic. Bored by routine, constantly seeks new challenges. Good at reading people.	Sarvepalli Radhakrishnan, Theodore Roosevelt, Rajkumar Hirani
ESTJ	Enforcer	Practical, decisive, organized. Focuses on efficiency, forceful in implementing plans.	Lakshmi Mittal, Michelle Obama, Ivanka Trump.
ESFJ	Helper	Warm-hearted and cooperative. Seeks harmony, completes tasks accurately and on time. Attuned to others' needs.	Lal Bahadur Shastri, Dr. B.R. Ambedkar, Prince William.

Type	Description	Characteristics	Famous Personalities
ENFJ	Sage	Warm, empathetic, responsible. Highly attuned to others' emotions. Acts as a catalyst for growth, provides inspiring leadership.	Preity Zinta, Dadasaheb Phalke, Oprah Winfrey.
ENTJ	Leader	Frank, decisive, assumes leadership readily. Logical, enjoys long-term planning. Forceful in presenting ideas.	Winston Churchill, Bill Gates, Dhirubhai Ambani.

THINGS TO CONSIDER WHILE DISCOVERING PERSONALITY TYPE:

- There is no superior personality type among the 16 types. Each type is unique and offers various career possibilities.
- The main aim of discovering personality types is to understand and appreciate differences between individuals.
- The MBTI personality type is sorted only by preferences. It doesn't measure a person's traits, abilities, habits, and character. These aspects should be addressed separately.

- It gives you an idea about your personality type, which helps you choose a suitable career option.
- If you find your personality and build a career based on that, you will love and enjoy your work, contributing to your happiness and health. Otherwise, you struggle in your career, ending up with dissatisfaction, frustration, limited growth, etc.
- You can conduct a short research to find out more about the career options in each type of personality.
- The information given in this chapter is for basic understanding on MBTI and how it works, for best results consult MBTI professional or, visit the following websites or explore other relevant websites or books.

    1. https://www.myersbriggs.org
    2. https://mbtionline.com
    3. https://www.16personalities.com
    4. http://www.humanmetrics.com

Despite knowing about personalities and the unique traits that forge our careers, children often deal with parents pressuring them to pursue a particular career option. While it can be argued that it is for the well-being of the child, such external pressures can often lead to adverse effects on mental health, causing stress and dissatisfaction in their student and professional lives. Besides personality, another aspect plays a significant role in career choice and satisfaction - one's interests and passions. Let's dive further into the importance of aligning career choices not only with personality traits but also with personal interests and passions to ensure a more fulfilling and rewarding professional journey.

Chapter 7

INTEREST OR PASSION

> ***"Find something you're passionate about and keep tremendously interested in it."***
>
> ***–Julia Child***

Since you were a child, some of you must have been interested in sports while others were better at academics. Some of you were interested in art, while others were fascinated by computers. Your interest is what you enjoy doing regularly. When you work on something tirelessly and actually enjoy your task, that is what we call an interest. Interest is when your attention or curiosity is particularly engaged by something. That *something* is your interest.

While interest is all about wanting to learn something, passion is a strong and barely controllable emotion that makes you feel excited about that something. Your passion can be anything that simultaneously challenges you and motivates you. It puts you to work effortlessly and pushes you to achieve that task with devotion and utmost dedication.

Interest and passion are used interchangeably when talking about careers. From here on, we will take interest as the point of discussion. Wherever you find an interest, it includes passion. Thus, let's discuss your interests.

If you can align your interests with your career, it will be more enjoyable and motivating. It will also increase the satisfaction level at work and enhance the potential for achieving career success.

How to Identify Your Interests:

- Let your emotions guide your interest.
- Ask yourself how you feel while doing an activity or task.
- Find the areas where you find fun and happiness.
- Find the activity that you do with complete effortlessness, concentration, and consistency.
- Find the areas where you engage for long hours without fatigue.
- Find the tasks for which you are ready to jump at any time with full dedication.
- Find out whether, after completing the task, you feel relaxed and rewarded.

Self-Assessment Tools:

Various self-assessment tools are available to help you understand more about your career interests. Among them, the most popular career assessment tool is John Holland's RIASEC Model. This model gives you six general personality types describing different areas of interest. Holland has labeled the six personality types as

1. R – Realistic (Doers)
2. I – Investigative (Thinkers)
3. A – Artistic (Creators)
4. S – Social (Helpers)
5. E – Enterprising (Persuaders)
6. C – Conventional (Organizers)

Personality Types	**Characteristics**	**Professions**
Realistic (Doers)	Like to work with things, assertive, competitive. Have athletic and mechanical abilities. Prefer working with objects, machines, tools, plants, animals, or outdoors. Focus on motor coordination, skill, and strength. Prefer concrete problem-solving approaches. Drawn to scientific and mechanical areas.	Engineers, Foresters, Opticians, Property Managers, Software Engineers, Dental Technicians, Mechanics, Carpenters, Electricians, Police Officers, Farm Managers, etc.
Investigative (Thinkers)	Like to observe, learn, investigate, analyze, evaluate, and solve problems. Prefer thinking	Physicians, Psychologists, Biologists, Economists,

Personality Types	**Characteristics**	**Professions**
	and observing over action. Enjoy organizing and understanding information rather than persuading. Drawn to working with data rather than people.	Geologists, Mathematicians, Chemists, Pharmacists, Statisticians, Veterinarians, Software Engineers, Professors, Computer Programmers, Medical Lab Technicians, Management Consultants, etc.
Artistic (Creators)	Like to work with ideas and things. Creative, innovative, open, original, sensitive, independent, and emotional. Rebel against structure and rules. Dislike tasks involving people and physical skills. Prefer unstructured settings using imagination and creativity.	Architects, Journalists, Writers/Editors, Actors, Attorneys, Librarians, Graphic Designers, Artists, Dancers, Advertising Directors, etc.

Personality Types	Characteristics	Professions
Social (Helpers)	Like to work with other people to enlighten, help, train, or cure them. Skilled with words. Drawn to seek close relationships and less apt to be intellectual or physical.	Teachers, Historians, Psychologists, Human Resource Professionals, Social Workers, Counselors, Trainers, Community Organizers, Hospital Administrators, Nurses, Dietitians, etc.
Enterprising (Persuaders)	Like to work with people, influencing, persuading, performing, leading, or managing for organizational goals or economic gain. Good talkers use this skill to lead and persuade. Drawn to high-power situations, value power, money, and status.	Politicians, Business Managers, Entrepreneurs, Financial Planners, Sales Representatives, Managers, CEOs, Lawyers/Attorneys, Bartenders, Stockbrokers, Real Estate Agents, Travel Agents, Food Service Managers, etc.
Conventional (Organizers)	Like to work with data, have clerical or numerical ability. Carry out tasks in detail or follow through	Accountants, Administrators, Business Managers, Insurance Managers, Tax

Personality Types	**Characteristics**	**Professions**
	on others' instructions. Like rules and regulations, emphasize self-control. Value structure, order, power, and status.	Consultants, Travel Agents, Actuaries, Bookkeepers, Computer Operators, Data Processors, Medical Records Technicians, Paralegals, etc.

FIND YOU INTEREST

You have to identify your main interest among the above six types of personalities and associated work environments and rank them per your preferences. Assign a score ranks from to 1 to 6 to each type according to your priority:

R = Realistic: _____.

I = Investigative: _____.

A = Artistic: _____.

S = Social: _____.

E = Enterprising: _____.

C = Conventional: _____.

Once you have determined your top three letters, record them under "My Interest Code."

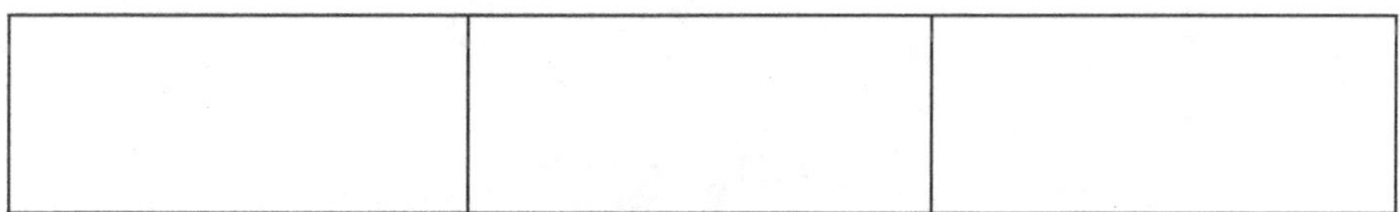

Understanding and aligning your career choices with your interests and passions is are essential to a fulfilling professional journey. Your unique personality traits and distinct interests contribute to overall job satisfaction and personal well-being. As we move on, you must note that a comprehensive approach to a career includes not only one's interests but also one's innate abilities and intelligence. Read on as we explore the intersection of aptitude and passion to provide you with a holistic view of career decision-making.

Chapter 8

APTITUDE AND INTELLIGENCE

Our journey toward a career often begins with passion and interest, the driving forces behind our pursuits. However, as human beings, our inherent aptitudes and intelligence also play a major role in shaping our career options. Sometimes, our potential can be constrained by these innate factors, limiting our possibilities. This chapter will uncover the importance of aptitude and intelligence in our career-making decisions and also how those alone should not limit us from achieving our potential. As you reach for the stars, you must realize that your abilities are directed by your enthusiasm to reach the feats once thought to be beyond your grasp.

APTITUDE

> ***"The winner's edge is not in a gifted birth, a high IQ, or in talent. The winner's edge is all in the attitude, not aptitude. Attitude is the criterion for success."***
>
> ***– Denis Waitley***

In various recruitment exams like UPSC, SSC, State Public Service Commissions, Banking, as well as in private companies for bulk recruitment, the aptitude test is mandatory to filter the candidates. That is why every student must be aware of their aptitude.

Aptitude refers to a natural or acquired capacity or ability. It is often used to describe a person's inherent talent or capacity in particular areas, such as language or music. While often compared to skills and abilities developed through learning, it's distinct.

Aptitude tests help to identify careers that are a good fit for their natural abilities, help students make informed decisions about their careers and education, help schools place students in classes that are challenging but not too difficult, and assist employers in identifying candidates who are likely to be successful in a particular job.

There are many types of aptitude tests, each designed to measure a specific area of ability. Some standard aptitude tests include:

- **Verbal aptitude tests:** These tests measure a person's ability to understand and use language.
- **Numerical aptitude tests:** These tests measure a person's ability to understand and use numbers.
- **Spatial aptitude tests:** These tests measure a person's ability to visualize and manipulate objects in space.
- **Mechanical aptitude tests:** These tests measure a person's ability to understand and work with machines.
- **Clerical aptitude tests:** These tests measure a person's ability to perform tasks such as filing, data entry, and following instructions.

HOW TO IMPROVE APTITUDE

If you want to enhance your aptitude, you can improve it through practice. The more you practice, the better you will be at solving aptitude test questions. There are many books and online resources that offer practice tests and questions. If you find a question difficult, don't give up; try to work through it or skip it and come back to it later. It is important to stay calm during the test. If you start feeling anxious, take a few deep breaths and refocus on the task at hand. Practice and composure are key to improving your aptitude.

INTELLIGENCE

> ***"Intelligence is not measured by how much you know, but by how much you have the capacity to learn."***
>
> ***— Francesca Zappia***

Intelligence is the ability to learn, understand, and apply knowledge effectively. It is also the ability to think abstractly, solve problems, and make decisions. Intelligence plays an important role in many areas of life, including school, work, and relationships. Individuals with high intelligence often excel at quickly grasping new concepts, solving problems efficiently, and making good decisions, contributing to success in academic, professional, and personal spheres.

Various theories attempt to explain intelligence, and one of the most popular ones is the theory of multiple intelligences, developed by Howard Gardner in 1983. Gardner proposed eight types of intelligence, each independent of the others. The eight types of intelligence are:

- **Linguistic intelligence:** The ability to use language effectively. People with high linguistic intelligence are good at reading, writing, and speaking. They are also good at understanding and using metaphors and analogies.

- **Logical-mathematical intelligence:** The ability to think logically and solve problems. People with high logical-mathematical intelligence are good at reasoning, calculating, and predicting. They are also good at understanding and using abstract concepts.

- **Spatial intelligence:** The ability to visualize and manipulate objects in space. People with high spatial intelligence are good at drawing, painting, and sculpting. They are also good at understanding and using maps and charts.

- **Bodily-kinesthetic intelligence:** The ability to use one's body to control objects and movements. People with high bodily-kinesthetic intelligence are good at dancing, playing sports, and performing physical tasks. They are also good at understanding and using their bodies to express themselves.

- **Musical intelligence:** The ability to appreciate and create music. People with high musical intelligence are good at singing, playing instruments, and composing music. They are also good at understanding and using rhythm and melody.

- **Interpersonal intelligence:** The ability to understand and interact with others. People with high interpersonal intelligence are good at communicating with others, understanding their feelings, and resolving conflicts. They are also good at working in groups and building relationships.

- **Intrapersonal intelligence:** The ability to understand oneself. People with high intrapersonal intelligence are good at understanding their own thoughts, feelings, and motivations. They are also good at setting goals and making decisions.

- **Naturalist intelligence:** The ability to understand and appreciate nature. People with high naturalist intelligence are good at identifying plants and animals, understanding ecosystems, and appreciating the beauty of nature.

There are many different ways to measure intelligence, such as IQ, achievement, and personality tests. IQ tests measure a person's overall intelligence, achievement tests measure a person's knowledge in a particular subject area, and personality tests measure a person's individual characteristics, such as their thinking style, learning style, and personality traits.

However, it is important to note that intelligence is not a fixed trait. It can change and grow over time. While intelligence is crucial, success is influenced by several other factors, like hard work, determination, and perseverance.

APTITUDE VS. INTELLIGENCE

Aptitude and intelligence, although often used interchangeably, are quite distinct from each other. Consider a story where two friends, Radha and Sita, decide to learn a new language. Radha has a natural aptitude for languages and effortlessly picks up nuances, pronunciation, and grammar. Her aptitude for linguistic skills is evident. On the other hand, Sita, though not naturally inclined, has an intense curiosity toward language learning. Her intelligence shows as she strategically learns the language, understands patterns, and applies logic. Through this, we get to realize that Radha's success reflects her aptitude, while Sita's achievement highlights her intelligence, showcasing that these two concepts bring distinct strengths to the table.

Here is a table summarizing the key differences between aptitude and intelligence:

Characteristic	**Aptitude**	**Intelligence**
Definition	A person's natural ability to learn or acquire a skill.	A person's overall mental ability.
Measurement	Aptitude tests	IQ tests
Specificity	More specific	Less specific
Usefulness for predicting success.	More useful for predicting success in a particular field.	More useful for predicting success in overall life.

It is important to note that both aptitude and intelligence are important factors that can contribute to a person's success in life. However, aptitude is more specific and useful for predicting success in a particular field.

While inherently, we possess certain qualities, our ability to learn is a unique factor that can help bridge the gap between our innate and acquired capabilities. Understanding how we naturally absorb and process information helps us gain a firmer foothold in our career journey. Just as aptitude and intelligence lay the foundation, learning style unveils the personalized approach through which we navigate the vast realms of knowledge.

Write down your three intelligences among the eight types of intelligence proposed by Gardner based on dominance.

1.

2.

3.

Chapter 9

LEARNING STYLE

"Every student can learn, just not on the same day, or the same way."

– George Evans

As a student, you've probably noticed that everyone has their unique way of learning. Learning style refers to the preferential way in which you absorb, process, comprehend, and retain information. It depends on various factors, such as cognitive, emotional, and environmental factors, as well as your past experiences. Some students like a theoretical approach to different concepts taught in class, while others might prefer a practical take.

Recognizing your unique learning style is important to improving your academic performance. This would help you move faster toward your dream career as it is beneficial for tackling entrance exams that are mandatory for many courses.

One of the most popular models for understanding learning styles is the "Dunn and Dunn" Learning Style, proposed by Dr. Rita Dunn and Dr. Kenneth Dunn.

DUNN AND DUNN LEARNING STYLE

Dunn and Dunn identify five key dimensions that can shape a student's learning style:

1. **Environmental:** It means where you prefer to get your learning. Is it in a calm and quiet place or somewhere with lots of pillows and mood lighting? Formal or informal environment?

2. **Emotional:** Do you require a lot of emotional support? Can you take individual responsibility, and what sorts of structures are helpful for you?

3. **Sociological:** Do you work best on your own, in pairs, or in a group? Or do you need guidance from adults or the instructor?

4. **Physiological:** How do you (in addition to the mind) respond to the learning task? Whether you are a visual, auditory, or kinesthetic learner.

5. **Psychological**: How do you process and respond to information and ideas? Are you analytical and good with numbers? Or global, preferring to see the big picture? Are you reflective, taking time to answer, or impulsive in shooting that hand up in the air?

Dunn and Dunn's Learning Style Dimensions

The Dunns Dunn and Dunn discuss five types of stimuli that can affect you and the elements that play into each stimulus to differentiate individual learners.

Dimension or Stimuli	**Elements**	**Key Questions**
Environment	Sound Light Temperature Seating Design	Do students prefer a noisy, busy, well-lit, warm environment or a quiet, subdued, more relaxed environment? Should the learning environment be formal (e.g., desks and chairs) or informal (e.g., pillows)?
Emotional	Motivational support. Persistence Individual Responsibility. Structure	Do students need a lot of emotional support? Will they persist in learning tasks? Can they assume individual responsibility? Do they need lots of structure?
Sociological	Individual Pairs or Teams Adult Varied	Do students learn best alone or working with someone? How much guidance from adults do they want or need?

Dimension or Stimuli	Elements	Key Questions
Physiological	Perceptual Intake Time Mobility	Is the student an auditory, visual, tactile, or kinesthetic learner? Does the student like to snack while learning? When is the optimal time for learning? Does the student require freedom to move during learning?
Psychological	Global Analytical Impulsive Reflective	How does the learner attack problems, globally or analytically? Does the student jump into problems or pause to reflect before starting?

Write Down Below. Based on the Table Above, What Fits Your Learning Style:

___

Note: Knowing your learning style allows you to understand what suits you best while learning things, and you can improve your academic performance accordingly.

The learning style does not help you to know what your career is that is the right fit for you. It just helps you to adapt learning styles to match different learning situations in your education and employment.

Knowingly or unknowingly, you must have used different learning styles to help you in your academic learning. While some students prefer to read out loud, others are silent readers and like to think more deeply about the topic. Some prefer to take notes while studying, others prefer to highlight. Also, some choose to listen to music as a learning stimulus, while others like to walk the length of the room to learn. No matter how many unique ways you employ to help you in your academic learning, it is more important to learn additional skills to help climb the career ladder. The 21st-century skills, in today's time, are the extra boost to your career journey that makes you an indispensable member of an organization.

Chapter 10

21ST CENTURY SKILLS

"No one can discover you until you do. Exploit your talents, skills, and strengths and make the world sit up and take notice."

– Rob Liano

Skill is the ability that allows you to do something well, often referred to as expertise. It is the ability to apply your knowledge effectively and readily in practical situations. For example, Communication skills, Leadership skills, Coding skills, Listening skills, Interpersonal skills, Computer skills, Customer service skills, and more fall under the broad category of skills.

These skills are helpful in different stages of career and life and can be divided into three parts:

1. **Personal Traits/Attitudes:** These involve characteristics required to perform work shaped by your life experience. E.g., to be independent, patient, diplomatic, result-oriented, resilient, etc.
2. **Knowledge-based Skills:** These skills involve having knowledge of a specific subject or procedure and the information necessary to perform a specific task

acquired through education. For example, your graduation majors include maths, science, accounting, management, etc.

3. **Functional/Transferable Skills:** These skills are relevant to actions taken to perform a task and are transferable to different work functions and industries based on your abilities and aptitude. They become particularly helpful as you enter the workforce. E.g., Writing skills, Analyzing skills, Organizing skills, Promoting skills, etc. Recognizing and developing these skills contributes significantly to your overall competence and success in both your personal and professional endeavors.

21ST CENTURY SKILLS

The 21st century is the age of technology and innovation, stringing and connecting the world closer than ever before. The rapid expansion of innovative ideas means that students today need to have the ability to think critically and have a creative mindset to flourish. There is no one definition for 21st-century skills. However, they constitute the very base of this new, technically advanced world. Today, having these skills is not an additional requirement but rather a necessity for students who want to have a successful career. It is also the means through which these students can become capable adults and members of society who can contribute to the development and progress of a nation. These 21st-century skills fall into three categories:

Learning Skills (4Cs): These are the skills required to gain new knowledge and include-

- **Critical Thinking:** Objective analysis, fairness, open-mindedness, informed, curious, problem-solving capability, and independence.
- **Creativity & Innovation:** Fluency, flexibility, originality, and elaboration in thinking creatively.
- **Collaboration:** Effective teamwork where you respect the thoughts of others and have common goals.
- **Communication:** Speaking one's thoughts, ideas, and wishes either orally or non-verbally.

Literacy Skills (IMT): These are skills that allow the acquisition of information through reading, media, and digital resources-

- **Information Literacy:** Finding and judging the quality of information.
- **Media Literacy:** Comprehending and dissecting media content.
- **Technology Literacy:** Navigating digital technologies appropriately to achieve the desired outcomes.

Life Skills (FLIPS): These are everyday skills essential for living a successful as well as a full life-

- **Flexibility and Adaptability:** Changing actions in response to new circumstances without compromising integrity.

- **Leadership and Responsibility:** Effective team management entails building personal qualities like loyalty, commitment, and resilience, among others.
- **Initiative and Self-Direction:** Begin tasks on your initiative.
- **Responsibility and Productivity:** Finishing assignments within deadlines set by others while feeling responsible for one's actions.
- **Social Interaction:** Communicating effectively in different social contexts.

To develop as an individual, it is essential to have a combination of all these skills, as they allow you to confront real-life hurdles with fortitude, inventiveness, and accountability. These capabilities not only make people better individuals but also serve to upgrade the whole learning process that will enable them to cope with technology and innovation in a world that is increasingly dynamic and interconnected.

STEP II: CAREER PATHWAY

The first step, getting to know yourself, lays a rock-solid foundation for your career and life. It becomes your guiding force, helping you navigate the many challenges life throws at you. With this foundation in place, step II involves constructing your ambitions and aspirations.

Similar to a building's foundation that stays strong amidst calamities, your career also needs a sturdy structure that aligns with your ambitions. Constructing a substantial and sustainable career requires relevant, quality education to focus on these four areas of impact. To scale the ladder of success, these four steps are irreplaceable:

1. **Selecting the Right Career:** Choose a path that aligns with your interests and strengths.
2. **Joining a Relevant Course:** Go for a course that directly relates to your career choice.
3. **Admission to a Suitable College:** Select a college that complements your educational goals.
4. **Studying in Your Dream Country:** If relevant, consider studying in a location that enhances your learning experience.

Achieving the above areas can be overwhelming and may involve many dilemmas and tough decisions. However, you must make an informed decision based on the vast amount of information available. At this stage, any mistake may impact various aspects of a successful career and life.

Chapter 11

SELECTING THE RIGHT CAREER

"Choosing the right career is the most difficult task for a person who is multi-talented and versatile. Because it's hard to decide what field to go into when you are good at too many things."

– Saad Salman

The first step of self-discovery has given you some idea of your inherent qualities and potential career paths. However, it did not suggest specific career options available for you. To make an informed decision, you must be aware of all the available career options. You have to consider all the resources, viz., finances, location, weather, community, campus life, scholarships, internships, part-time jobs, and employment opportunities available when selecting courses.

Selecting a career from the wide range of options available will ensure greater satisfaction and confidence. Limited options, in this case, lead to future disappointment. Knowing more options brings clarity, paving the way for a happier and healthier career and life.

The basis of selecting the right career is aligning it with your interests. There are two types of career interests:

1. Primary Career Interest.
2. Secondary Career Interest.

The Primary and Secondary career interests guide you in selecting the right Major and Minor subjects in college.

Following is a probable list of career interests:

1. Being creative and innovative
2. Communicating with people
3. Designing and styling
4. Helping and guiding people
5. Media, glamour, and entertainment
6. Nature and outdoors
7. Observing human behaviour
8. Organising and structuring
9. Physical activity
10. Playing with numbers
11. Solving problems
12. Taking risks
13. Technology and gadgets.
14. Working with hands, machines, and tools

Select your first and second preferences from the list and write them down. These preferences will guide you in exploring potential career options aligned with your interests.

First Preference/Primary Interest:

____

Second Preference/Secondary Interest:

____

Explore the possible career options below, matching your primary and secondary interests. You may consider them for your future career. Identify the section that resonates most with you and note it down for future reference.

I. Being Creative and Innovative:

Primary Interest	Secondary Interest	Probable Careers
Being Creative and Innovative	Communicating with people.	Fine Arts
	Designing and Styling	1. Fine Arts 2. Architecture 3. Automotive Engineering 4. Visual Communication 5.Game Design 6.Fasion Design
	Media, Glamour, and Entertainment	1. Animation 2. Fashion Designing

Primary Interest	Secondary Interest	Probable Careers
	Nature and Outdoors	1. Architecture 2. Mass Communication and Journalism
	Observing Human Behavior	1. Fine Arts 2. Animation 3. Blogger/Writer 4. Psychology
	Organizing and Structuring	1. Fine Arts
	Physical Activity	1. Civil Engineering
	Playing with Numbers	1. Architecture 2. Game Designer
	Solving Problems	1. Automobile Designing 2. Business Management 3. Computer Applications 4. Automotive Engineering 5. Biomedical 6. Biotechnology
	Taking Risks	1. Business Management
	Technology and Gadgets.	1. Computer Applications 2. Visual Communication

Primary Interest	Secondary Interest	Probable Careers
		3. Biotechnology 4. Animation 5. Game Design
	Working with Hands, Machines, and Tools	1. Fine Arts 2. Civil Engineering 3. Automotive Engineering

II. Communicating with People:

Primary Interest	Secondary Interest	Probable Careers
Communicating with People	Being Creative and Innovative	1. Fine Arts 2. Youtuber/Vlogger
	Helping and Guiding People	1. Teaching 2. Pharmacy 3. Hotel Management 4. Law 5. Linguistics 6. Psychology
	Media, Glamour, and Entertainment	1. Hotel Management 2. Mass Communication and Journalism
	Nature and Outdoors	1. Travel and Tourism 2. Mass Communication and Journalism

Primary Interest	Secondary Interest	Probable Careers
	Observing Human Behavior	1. Law 2. Psychology
	Organizing and Structuring	1. Company Secretaryship. 2. Business Management 3. Pharmacy 4. Travel and Tourism 5. Chartered Accountancy
	Physical Activity	1.Physiotherapy
	Solving Problems	1. Business Management 2. Law
	Taking Risks	1. Business Management 2. Digital Marketing 3. Air Hostess 4. Mass Communication and Journalism 5. Law 6. Medicine

III. Designing and Styling:

Primary Interest	Secondary Interest	Probable Careers
Designing and Styling	Being Creative and Innovative	1. Fine Arts 2. Architecture

Primary Interest	**Secondary Interest**	**Probable Careers**
		3. Automotive Engineering 4. Visual Communication 5. Game Design 6. Fasion Designing
	Media, Glamour, and Entertainment	1.Fashion Designing
	Nature and Outdoors	1. Fine Arts 2. Architecture
	Observing Human Behavior	1. Fine Arts 2. Architecture
	Organizing and Structuring	1. Fashion Designing
	Playing with Numbers	1. Architecture 2. Game Design
	Solving Problems	1. Computer Applications 2. Automotive Engineering 3. Game Design
	Technology and Gadgets.	1. Visual Communication 2. Game Design
	Working with Hands, Machines, and Tools	1.Fine Arts 2. Automotive Engineering 3. Fashion Designing

IV. Help and Guidance:

Primary Interest	Secondary Interest	Probable Careers
Help and Guiding	Communicating with People	1.Teaching 2. Pharmacy 3. Dietician & Nutritionist 4. Hotel Management 5. Law 6. Linguistics 7. Psychology
	Media, Glamour, and Entertainment	1. Hotel Management 2. Mass Communication and Journalism
	Nature and Outdoors	1. Hotel Management 2. Travel and Tourism 3.Air Hostess
	Observing Human Behavior	1.Psychology
	Organizing and Structuring	1.Pharmacy
	Physical Activity	1.Defence
	Playing with Numbers	1. Chartered Accountancy

Primary Interest	**Secondary Interest**	**Probable Careers**
	Solving Problems	1.Physiotherapy 2.Law 3.Dentistry 4.Medicine 5.Biomedical
	Taking Risks	1.Defence 2.Law 3.Medicine
	Working with Hands, Machines, and Tools	1.Physiotherapy 2.Dentistry

V. Media, Glamour, and Entertainment:

Primary Interest	**Secondary Interest**	**Probable Careers**
Media, Glamour, and Entertainment	Being Creative and Innovative	1. Sports Journalism 2. Animation 3. Fashion Designing
	Communicating with people.	1. Hotel Management 2. Mass Communication and Journalism
	Designing and Styling	1. Fasion Designing

Primary Interest	Secondary Interest	Probable Careers
	Helping and Guiding People	1. Hotel Management 2. Mass Communication and Journalism
	Nature and Outdoors	1. Mass Communication and Journalism
	Observing Human Behavior	No matches in this category.
	Organizing and Structuring	1. Mass Communication and Journalism
	Physical Activity	No matches in this category.
	Playing with Numbers	1. Game Designer
	Solving Problems	1. Law
	Taking Risks	1. Mass Communication and Journalism
	Technology and Gadgets	1. Animation 2. Game Design
	Working with Hands, Machines, and Tools.	1. Fine Arts 2. Fashion Technology

VI. Nature and Outdoors:

Primary Interest	Secondary Interest	Probable Careers
Nature and Outdoors	Being Creative and Innovative	1. Architecture

Primary Interest	Secondary Interest	Probable Careers
		2. Mass Communication and Journalism
	Communicating with people.	1. Travel and Tourism 2. Mass Communication and Journalism
	Designing and Styling	1. Fine Arts 2. Architecture
	Helping and Guiding People	1. Hotel Management 2. Travel and Tourism
	Media, Glamour, and Entertainment	1. Mass Communication and Journalism
	Organizing and Structuring	1. Travel and Tourism
	Physical Activity	No matches in this category.
	Playing with Numbers	1.Architecture
	Taking Risks	1. Mass Communication and Journalism
	Technology and Gadgets.	No matches in this category.
	Working with Hands, Machines, and Tools	1.Civil Engineering 2. Mining and Geological Engineering

VII. Observing Human Behaviour:

Primary Interest	Secondary Interest	Probable Careers
Observing Human Behavior	Being Creative and Innovative	1. Fine Arts 2. Animation 3. Psychology
	Communicating with people.	1. Luxury Brands Manager 2. Law 3. Psychology
	Designing and Styling	1. Fine Arts 2. Animation
	Helping and Guiding People	1. Psychology
	Media, Glamour, and Entertainment	No matches in this category.
	Organizing and Structuring	1. Psychology
	Solving Problems	1. Criminal Investigations and Special Agents 2. Law 3. Psychology
	Taking Risks	1. Psychology
	Working with Hands, Machines, and Tools	1. Animation

VIII. Organising and Structuring:

Primary Interest	Secondary Interest	Probable Careers
Organizing and Structuring	Being Creative and Innovative	1. Fine Arts 2. Wedding Planner
	Communicating with people.	1. Company Secretaryship. 2. Business Management 3. Pharmacy 4. Travel and Tourism 5. Chartered Accountancy
	Designing and Styling	1. Fashion Designing
	Helping and Guiding People	1. Pharmacy
	Media, Glamour, and Entertainment	1. Mass Communication and Journalism
	Nature and Outdoors	1. Travel and Tourism
	Observing Human Behavior	1. Psychology
	Physical Activity	No matches in this category.
	Playing with Numbers	1. Actuarial Sciences 2. Company Secretaryship 3. Banking and Insurance

Primary Interest	Secondary Interest	Probable Careers
		4. Chartered Accountancy
	Solving Problems	1. Actuarial Sciences 2. Company Secretaryship 3. Business Management 4. Chartered Accountancy
	Taking Risks	1. Company Secretaryship. 2. Business Management 3. Chartered Accountancy
	Technology and Gadgets.	No matches in this category.
	Working with Hands, Machines, and Tools	No matches in this category.

IX. Physical Activity:

Primary Interest	Secondary Interest	Probable Careers
Physical Activity	Being Creative and Innovative	1. Civil Engineering
	Communicating with people.	1. Physiotherapy

Primary Interest	**Secondary Interest**	**Probable Careers**
	Helping and Guiding People	1.Defence
	Media, Glamour, and Entertainment	No matches in this category.
	Nature and Outdoors	1. Mining and Geological Engineering
	Organizing and Structuring	1. Sports Management
	Playing with Numbers	1. Mechanical Engineering
	Solving Problems	1. Mechanical Engineering. 2. Aeronautical Engineering 3. Defence 4. Physio Therapy
	Taking Risks	1.Defence
	Technology and Gadgets.	1. Aeronautical Engineering
	Working with Hands, Machines, and Tools	1. Civil Engineering 2. Mechanical Engineering 3. Mining and Geological Engineering 4. Aeronautical Engineering

X. Playing with Numbers:

Primary Interest	Secondary Interest	Probable Careers
Playing with Numbers	Being Creative and Innovative	1. Architecture 2. Accounancy (ACCA)
	Designing and Styling	1.Architecture 2. Games Design
	Helping and Guiding People	1. Chartered Accountancy
	Media, Glamour, and Entertainment	1. Game Design
	Nature and Outdoors	1. Architecture
	Organizing and Structuring	1. Actuarial Sciences 2. Company Secretaryship 3. Banking and Insurance 4. Chartered Accountancy 5. Forensic Accounting 6. Accountancy (ACCA)
	Physical Activity	1. Mechanical Engineering
	Solving Problems	1. Actuarial Sciences 2. Company Secretaryship 3. Banking and Insurance 4. Chartered Accountancy 5. Accountancy (ACCA)

Primary Interest	**Secondary Interest**	**Probable Careers**
		6. Stock Broker 7. Mechanical Engineer 8. Computer Engineer
	Taking Risks	1. Business Management 2. Banking and Insurance
	Technology and Gadgets.	1. Computer Applications 2. Electrical Engineering 3. Computer Engineering 4. Games Design
	Working with Hands, Machines, and Tools	1. Electrical Engineering 2. Mechanical Engineering

XI. Solving Problems:

Primary Interest	**Secondary Interest**	**Probable Careers**
Solving Problems	Being Creative and Innovative	1. Business Management 2. Computer Application 3. Automotive Engineering 4. Biomedical 5. Biotechnology
	Communicating with people.	1. Business Management 2. Business Analyst 3. Law

Primary Interest	**Secondary Interest**	**Probable Careers**
	Designing and Styling	1. Computer Applications 2. Automotive Engineering 3. Games Design
	Helping and Guiding People	1.Physiotherapy 2. Law 3. Dentistry 4. Medicine
	Media, Glamour, and Entertainment	1. Law
	Observing Human Behavior	1. Criminal Investigations and Special Agents 2. Law 3. Psychology
	Organizing and Structuring	1. Actuarial Sciences 3. Busniness Management 4. Chartered Accountancy
	Physical Activity	1. Mechanical Engineering. 2. Aeronautical Engineering 3. Defence 4. Physiotherapy

Primary Interest	**Secondary Interest**	**Probable Careers**
	Playing with Numbers	1. Actuarial Sciences 2. Company Secretaryship 3. Chartered Accountancy 4. Banking and Insurance 5. Mechanical Engineering 6. Computer Engineering
	Taking Risks	1. Business Management 2. Defense 3. Law 4. Medicine
	Technology and Gadgets.	1. Computer Applications 2. Electrical Engineering 3. Computer Engineering 4. Aeronautical Engineering 5. Biotechnology.
	Working with Hands, Machines, and Tools	1. Chemical Engineering. 2. Electrical Engineering 3. Mechanical Engineering 4. Automotive Engineering 5.Aeronautical Engineering

XII. Taking Risks:

Primary Interest	Secondary Interest	Probable Careers
Taking Risks	Being Creative and Innovative	1. Business Management
	Communicating with people.	1. Business Management 2. Mass Communication and Journalism 3. Law 4. Medicine
	Helping and Guiding People	1. Defence 2. Law 3. Medicine 4. Accountancy (ACCA)
	Media, Glamour, and Entertainment	1. Mass Communication and Journalism
	Nature and Outdoors	1. Mass Communication and Journalism
	Observing Human Behavior	1.Psychology
	Organizing and Structuring	1. Company Secretaryship 2. Busniness Management 3. Chartered Accountancy
	Physical Activity	1. Defence
	Playing with Numbers	1. Business Management 2. Banking and Insurance 3. Accountancy (ACCA)

Primary Interest	**Secondary Interest**	**Probable Careers**
	Solving Problems	1. Business Management
		2. Investment Banking
		3. Accountancy (ACCA)
		4. Defence
		5. Law
		6. Medicine
	Technology and Gadgets.	1. Defence
	Working with Hands, Machines, and Tools	No matches in this category.

XIII. Technology and Gadgets:

Primary Interest	**Secondary Interest**	**Probable Careers**
Technology and Gadgets	Being Creative and Innovative	1. Computer Applications 2. Visual Communications 3. Biotechnology 4. Animation 5. Games Design
	Designing and Styling	1. Visual Communications 2. Games Designing
	Media, Glamour, and Entertainment	1. Animation 2. Games Designing

Primary Interest	Secondary Interest	Probable Careers
	Nature and Outdoors	No matches in this category
	Physical Activity	1. Aeronautical Engineering
	Playing with Numbers	1. Computer Applications 2. Electrical Engineering 3. Computer Engineering 4. Games Design
	Solving Problems	1. Computer Applications 2. App Development 3. Website Designing 4. Electrical Engineering 5. Computer Engineering 6. Aeronautical Engineering 7. Biotechnology
	Taking Risks	1.Defence
	Working with Hands, Machines, and Tools	1.Data Architect 2. Civil Engineering 3. Electrical Engineering 4. Mechanical Engineering 5. Mining and Geological Engineering 6. Aeronautical Engineering

XIV. Working with Hands, Machines, and Tools:

Primary Interest	Secondary Interest	Probable Careers
Working with Hands, Machines, and Tools	Being Creative and Innovative	1. Fine Arts 2. Civil Engineering 3. Automotive Engineering
	Designing and Styling	1. Fine Arts 2. Automotive Engineering 3. Fashion Designing
	Helping and Guiding People	1. Physiotherapy 2. Dentistry
	Media, Glamour, and Entertainment	1. Fine Arts 2. Fashion Designing
	Nature and Outdoors	1.Civil Engineering 2. Mining and Geological Engineering
	Observing Human Behavior	1.Animation
	Organizing and Structuring	1.Data Scientist
	Physical Activity	1.Astronaut 2. Civil Engineering 3. Mechanical Engineering

Primary Interest	Secondary Interest	Probable Careers
		4. Mining and Geological Engineering 5. Aeronautical Engineering
	Playing with Numbers	1. Electrical Engineering
	Solving Problems	1. Chemical Engineering. 2. Electrical Engineering 3. Mechanical Engineering 4. Automotive Engineering 5. Aeronautical Engineering 6. Dentistry
	Taking Risks	No matches in this category.
	Technology and Gadgets.	1. Civil Engineering 2. Electrical Engineering 3. Mechanical Engineering 4. Mining and Geological Engineering 5. Aeronautical Engineering

Write down your Probable Career Options as per your priority:

1. ______________________________

2. ______________________________

3. ______________________________

4. ______________________________

5. ______________________________

Chapter 12

COURSE

"Life presents many choices; the choices we make determine our future."

– Catherine Pulsifer

When you're in the schooling phase, crucial decisions await, varying for 9th and 10th-grade students and 11th and 12th-grade students. Two distinct stages involve two critical choices:

1. Choosing the Right Stream/Majors.
2. Planning the Right Career Option.

Throughout these stages, students undergo four common dilemmas:

1. Confusion about Career and Stream Options.
2. Clarity on Stream Choice but Confused about Career Options.
3. Confused about Stream Option but Clear about Career Options.
4. Clear about Stream and Career Option but Seeking Validation or Information on Specialisations

Some students base their career choices on subjects they enjoy in their school days, while others have specific career aspirations, such as becoming a doctor, engineer, pilot, etc., and choose their stream accordingly. Both approaches are correct, but achieving clarity is crucial. If they are in a dilemma until the completion of the 12th grade, their entire career may be in jeopardy. Immense stress, effort, time, and resources will be required to correct the dilemma and gain clarity.

Streams

Streams represent teaching branches available to the students, each leading to specific careers.

Choosing streams occurs at two levels in the K-12 education system:

1. After 10th Grade.
2. After 12th Grade.

After 10th Class

After completing the 10th grade, you will have the following option for continuing your studies:

1. Intermediate or 10+2.
2. Polytechnic.
3. ITI
4. Vocational Courses.

Intermediate or 10+2:

Intermediate or 10+2 is a two-year course leading to admissions into various degree courses, including professional courses like engineering and medicine, and academic courses like B.Sc., B.Com, and B.A., based on your chosen stream in 10+2 or intermediate. Three broad streams are common across boards:

1. Science Stream
2. Commerce Stream
3. Arts/Humanities Stream

Each stream has distinct methodologies, subject choices, and career options. Selection of a stream is an important decision that requires selecting the stream that aligns with your interests, goals, and skills. Here's an overview of each stream:

Science Stream

The science stream is mainly based on the theory and application of scientific concepts and experiments. Divided into Medical (P.C.B - Physics, Chemistry, and Biology) and Non-medical (P.C.M - Physics, Chemistry, and Mathematics) groups, this stream opens avenues in various fields.

1. Physics

Physics is among the oldest academic fields in the world and is the science of matter, motion, energy, and force. It focuses on understanding how the universe behaves. It explores matter, motion, energy, and force, providing observation, analysis, investigation, and decision-making skills. Career options include physicist, astronaut, data scientist, technician, and engineer.

2. Chemistry

Everything in the universe is made out of atoms and matter, and the study of Chemistry is based on the study of the composition, properties, and structure of matter, including atomic structure and the changes influenced by chemical reactions.

Career options include working in research, pharmaceuticals, and healthcare as lab scientists, chemical engineers, biochemists, flavor chemists, analytical chemists, etc.

3. Biology

Biology studies living organisms – plants and animals – including facets such as their physical structures, physiological mechanisms, chemical processes, molecular interactions, and development and evolution.

Career opportunities are immense, including the most popular path of medicine, which is MBBS, Ayurveda, or Homeopathy. Apart from medicine, it includes options such as biotechnology, dentistry, veterinary sciences, pharmaceuticals, botany, zoology, marine biology, genetics, bioinformatics, microbiology, and more.

4. Mathematics

Mathematics is a science of numbers and is often the most hated subject for students. It is sometimes the most loved subject for use in money transactions and applications, even in architecture, art, engineering, and sports. As a subject, Math focuses on the concepts of quantity, change, structure, and space. Career options include engineering, computer science, insurance, statistics, economics, banking, and accountancy.

Commerce Stream

Choosing the Commerce stream after 10th grade can open up a wide range of opportunities for you. Subjects are:

Accountancy: Understanding financial transactions and maintaining financial records.

Business Studies: Learning about business operations, management, and entrepreneurship.

Economics: Studying the economy, market dynamics, and economic policies.

Mathematics: Often included to enhance analytical and problem-solving skills.

Informatics Practices: Learning about computer applications and information technology.

Commerce stream offers flexibility, practical knowledge, and a strong foundation for various professional courses and careers like Chartered Accountancy (CA), Company Secretary (CS), Bachelor of Commerce (B.Com), Bachelor of Business Administration (BBA), Law (LLB), Economics (BA/BSc Economics), finance and Banking, Marketing, and Human Resources etc.

Arts/Humanities Stream

Choosing the Arts/Humanities stream after 10th grade can be a great decision if you have an interest in subjects like literature, history, and social sciences. Subjects are:

History: Study of past events and their impact on the present and future.

Geography: Understanding the physical features of the Earth and human-environment interactions.

Political Science: Learning about political systems, governance, and public policies.

Psychology: Study of human behavior and mental processes.

Sociology: Examination of society, social institutions, and social relationships.

Languages: English, Hindi, and other regional or foreign languages.

Economics: Basics of economic theories and practices.

The Arts/Humanities stream offers a wide range of career opportunities in Journalism and Mass Communication, Law (LLB), Teaching and Academia, Civil Services, Social Work, Public Administration, Creative Arts (Fine Arts, Performing Arts), Psychology and Counseling.

Selecting the right stream sets the stage for future academic and career pursuits. You must make informed decisions based on your interests and aspirations.

After 12th

Choosing the right career path after completing the 12th grade is an important decision, and seeking expert advice is essential to avoid future dissatisfaction. Here's an overview of popular career options for science students:

Engineering: It is the most popular and chosen career option, favored by parents across India. Every year, about 15 lakh engineers graduate, according to AICTE. Engineering can be pursued if you opt for PCM after the 12th.

List of Career Options in Engineering

- Computer Science
- Civil Engineering
- Mechanical Engineering
- Electrical Engineering
- Electronics & Communication
- Biotechnology
- Aeronautical Engineering
- Automobile Engineering
- Chemical Engineering
- Robotics Engineering

I would highly recommend you seek career guidance and counseling to have a better understanding of your career.

Before I move on to the New Age Career options, I would like to share one statistic that can help you plan your career. It is not meant to discourage you but rather serve as a reality check.

> ***"As per Times of India, 99% of all candidates fail in medical entrance exams every year and 99.2% fail to reach the top IITs."***

This statistic helps us realize that engineering or medicine is not everything, and it is possible to pursue an amazing career with the help of the right career guidance and advice.

New Age Career Options for Maths-Science Students

With the advent of technology, several new-age career options have emerged in the last decade.

- Artificial Intelligence & Machine Learning
- Data Analytics
- Big Data
- Data Science
- Ethical Hacking
- Robotics
- Aerospace
- Cybersecurity
- Physicists & Teaching

- Blockchain Engineer
- Game coder

You can choose a conventional career or opt for a new-age career. Career counseling can provide clarity in navigating these new-age choices.

Medical:

The general preconceived notion in a traditional Indian family is if it's a boy, then 'engineer', and if it's a girl, a 'doctor'. After engineering, the second most popular career path is medical.

Students with an interest in biology and a desire to become a doctor can choose this stream.

List of Career Options in Medical:

- MBBS
- BDS
- BAMS (Ayurveda)
- BHMS (Homeopathy)
- Bachelor of Pharmacy
- Bachelor of Physiotherapy
- Nursing
- Biotechnology
- BSc (Botany, Zoology, Nursing, Radiography)

- Bachelor of Occupational Therapy
- Food and Agriculture Science
- Ecologist.

New Age Career Options for Bio Students

- Sports Physiotherapy.
- Health care management.
- Health tourism.
- Dietitian
- Biomedical engineering.
- Biotechnologist
- Bioinformatics.
- Neuroinformatics
- Cognitive Neuroscience.
- Bachelor of Naturopathy & Yogic Science (BNYS)
- Environmental Science and Sustainable Development.
- Optometry.
- Audiology
- Clinical research.
- Hospital Management.

It's essential to recognize that traditional career paths like engineering and medicine are not the only routes to success. New-age options provide exciting prospects. Seeking timely career guidance ensures a well-informed decision that aligns with individual interests and goals, setting the foundation for a fulfilling career.

Career Options & Courses After 12th for Commerce:

Commerce is also considered to be one of the most popular career options.

List of Career Options in Commerce:

- B.Com (Hons)
- BBA – Finance
- BA (Hons) in Economics
- BBA/LLB
- BBA/BMS
- B.C.A (IT & Software)
- Chartered Accountant (CA)
- Cost Accountant
- Company Secretary (CS)
- B.Com/LLB
- Bachelor's in a foreign language
- Financial Analyst

- Banking
- Economist

Determining if commerce is suitable for you requires career advice from skilled and trained professionals. Many students seek to turn to career counseling to find their most suitable career path.

New Age Career Options for Commerce Students:

- Risk Management Analyst
- Budget Analyst
- Actuarial Science
- CMA
- Auditing
- Tax Consulting
- Corporate Strategist
- Wealth Management
- Private Equity & Venture Capital
- Certified Financial Analyst
- Stockbroking
- Investment analyst

Every new-age career option is an opportunity to explore your skills and interests. However, don't make any decision in haste. Career advice from an expert can help you make a wise career decision.

Career Options & Courses After 12th for Arts

In recent years, the perception of arts as a less popular stream has altered, opening up numerous lucrative career opportunities for students.

List of Career Options for Arts Students:

- BMS (Bachelor of Management Science)
- BFA (Bachelor of Fine Arts)
- BEM (Bachelor of Event Management)
- BBA (Bachelor of Business Administration)
- BFD (Bachelor of Fashion Design)
- Animation & Multimedia
- BBS (Bachelor of Business Studies)
- Bachelor of Performing Arts
- Sociology
- Psychology
- Photography
- Hotel/Hospital Management
- Catering
- Travel and Tourism

- Fashion Design
- Interior Design
- Communication Design
- Culinary Arts
- Journalism
- Animation
- Event Management
- Retail and Fashion Merchandise
- Teacher Training
- Textile Designing
- Sculpture
- Acting
- Air Hostess
- Artistic Basic Jewellery Design

New Age Career Options for Arts Students:

- Liberal Arts
- Sound Design
- App Design
- Graphical Design
- Visual merchandiser

- Content writer
- Social Media Management
- Fashion Styling
- Radio Jockey

This long list of new-age career options aims to provide clarity rather than confusion, offering a future to explore various career paths available to art students.

Polytechnic Course

Polytechnic Courses are an excellent choice for those eager to take up technical education after completing their 10th grade. Polytechnic colleges offer 1-3 years diploma courses in Engineering subjects like civil engineering, Mechanical Engineering, Computer Engineering, Automobile Engineering, Electronics and Instrumentation Engineering, and Pharmacy, etc. Upon completion of the diploma Course in Polytechnic Colleges, graduates can apply for supervisory level jobs in Government Engineering Departments and relevant private companies.

List of Polytechnic Courses:

- Computer Science and Engineering
- Civil Engineering
- Automobile Engineering.
- Electronics and Communication

- Electrical Engineering
- Interior Decoration
- Fashion Engineering
- Ceramic Engineering
- Art and Craft
- Mechanical Engineering
- Chemical Engineering
- Instrumentation and Control Engineering
- IT Engineering.
- Electronics and Telecommunication Engineering
- Aeronautical Engineering
- Petroleum Engineering
- Aerospace Engineering
- Mining Engineering
- Automobile Engineering.
- Genetic Engineering
- Biotechnology Engineering
- Plastics Engineering
- Agricultural Engineering
- Food Processing and Technology

- Dairy Technology and Engineering.
- Power Engineering.
- Infrastructure Engineering.
- Production Engineering
- Metallurgical Engineering
- Motorsport Engineering.
- Environmental Engineering
- Textile Engineering

Graduates can also pursue further education and join Engineering Courses like B.E., B.Tech, etc., through lateral entry into the 2nd year via a separate entrance exam.

- Indian Army
- GAIL – Gas Authority of India Limited
- DRDO – Defence Research and Development Organization
- ONGC – Oil and Natural Gas Corporation
- BHEL – Bharat Heavy Electricals Limited
- BSNL – Bharat Sanchar Nigam Limited
- NTPC – National Thermal Power Corporation
- IPCL – Indian Petro Chemicals Limited
- NSSO – National Sample Survey Organisation

- Jobs in Indian Railways
- Jobs in Public Works Departments
- Jobs in Infrastructure Development Agencies
- Jobs in Irrigation Departments

Similarly, many public sector companies also offer numerous job opportunities to graduates of polytechnic courses.

I.T.I (Industrial Training Institute)

Industrial Training Institutes, accredited by NCVET (National Council for Vocational Education and Training), offer diploma courses lasting 1-3 years and provide training in various trades like electrician, fitter, mechanical, and civil draftsmen.

Name of the Course	Stream	Duration
Tool & Die Maker Engineering	Engineering	3 years
Draftsman (Mechanical) Engineering	Engineering	2 years
Diesel Mechanic Engineering	Engineering	1 year
Draftsman (Civil) Engineering	Engineering	2 years
Pump Operator	Engineering	1 year
Fitter Engineering	Engineering	2 years

Name of the Course	Stream	Duration
Motor Driving-cum-Mechanic Engineering	Engineering	1 year
Turner Engineering	Engineering	2 years
Dress Making	Non-engineering	1 year
Manufacture Footwear	Non-engineering	1 year
Information Technology & E.S.M. Engineering	Engineering	2 years
Secretarial Practice	Non-engineering	1 year
Machinist Engineering	Engineering	1 year
Hair & Skin Care	Non-engineering	1 year
Refrigeration Engineering	Engineering	2 years
Fruit & Vegetable Processing	Non-engineering	1 year
Mechanical Instrumentation Engineering	Engineering	2 years
Bleaching & Dyeing Calico Print	Non-engineering	1 year
Electrician Engineering	Engineering	2 years
Letter Press Machine Mender	Non-engineering	1 year
Commercial Art	Non-engineering	1 year
Leather Goods Maker	Non-engineering	1 year

Name of the Course	Stream	Duration
Mechanic Motor Vehicle Engineering	Engineering	2 years
Hand Compositor	Non-engineering	1 year
Mechanic Radio & T.V. Engineering	Engineering	2 years
Mechanical Electronics Engineering	Engineering	2 years
Surveyor Engineering	Engineering	2 years
Foundry Man Engineering	Engineering	1 year
Sheet Metal Worker Engineering	Engineering	1 year

Vocational and Paramedical Courses

Vocational Junior Colleges offer courses equivalent to intermediate or 10+2 in various vocational and paramedic fields. These courses provide a bridge to degree programs for those continuing their education or serve as a pathway to employment for those entering the workforce directly. Some of the courses available include:

- DMLT (Diploma in Medical Lab Technology).
- DOA (Diploma in Ophthalmic Assistance)
- Accounts and Taxation
- Computer Applications
- Office Assistantship and more

To learn more about these courses and how to enroll, inquire locally for admission details.

Conclusion

After considering all the options available after 10th or 12th, what will be your choices?

After the 10th class.

1. ____________________
2. ____________________

After 12th Class.

1. ____________________
2. ____________________

Chapter 13

COLLEGE

"College is like a fountain of knowledge, and the students are there to drink."

– Chuck Palahniuk

Thinking about college or university can be overwhelming. College planning is a crucial step that can significantly impact your career. Selecting the right course and institution is vital for your future. Involving your parents in this process can be helpful.

It's best to start planning for your college early, preferably in 9th or 10th grade. This allows you to understand the process better and prepare adequately. Early planning helps you meet requirements like entrance exams, extracurricular activities, and financial preparations, reducing last-minute stress. In India, the concept of college typically comes after completing the 12th grade.

The college exploration process may be different at two levels.

1. At 9th and 10th Grades.

2. At 11th and 12th Grades.

At 9th and 10th Grades

The students at this stage are not ready to fully grasp the idea of college. The role of parents is crucial at this stage to help them navigate. Early exploration offers several benefits:

- Sets students on the right track early.
- Can have more ideas and concepts about colleges sooner
- Helps shape classes and activities for smoother transitions to 11th grade.
- Allows identification of preliminary interests in potential majors.
- Best time to explore and experiment with summer activities to prepare for 11th grade.

The college exploration process during 9th or 10th grades involves researching majors and subjects of interest. Steps include visiting college websites, exploring majors, taking virtual tours, and noting down research findings.

At 11th and 12th Grades

At this stage, the students are ready and interested in more in-depth exploration. It's time to narrow down college choices to 5 to 10 institutions. Academic performance and interest indicate a student's preference. For example, if the student excels in math and science, engineering would be the ideal choice. Shortlisting colleges based on academic profiles and career goals is essential.

Factors to Consider When Selecting Colleges:

Several factors should be considered when selecting a college besides rankings and brands:

1. **Education Programme:** The students must ensure the relevance of the education programme to industry needs and future studies. To ensure this, the students can visit colleges and speak to students studying there.
2. **Faculty:** Students have to ensure the availability of the best faculty in the college.
3. **Location:** It is a highly important factor because the student's inability to adapt to the college environment is a major dropout factor. Transportation also plays an important role.
4. **Weather:** Weather conditions where the college is located are important. It is difficult to spend 3 or 4 years in an unfamiliar weather condition, worsening homesickness and stress.
5. **Environment:** Here, environment refers to the rural, urban, or suburban environment, which is an essential factor to consider.
6. **Culture:** It is important to make friends and connections that will last a lifetime. If students find social groups with similar interests and values, they will be happy.
7. **Campus Life:** The campus life should be exciting for the students. They have to consider the time spent

outside the classroom in extracurricular activities like sports, student clubs, gym, lawns, and playgrounds, etc.

8. **Campus Safety:** Campus Safety is also one of the key factors when selecting a college, especially for girls. If required, the students must investigate the neighborhood around the campus.

9. **Cost of Education and Living:** It is one of the key factors. Costs include tuition fees, books, boarding and lodging, transportation, etc. The costs should be calculated for the entire 3 or 4 years of college and the scholarship availability.

10. **Placement Facility:** The students should check for the placement data on the college website. The students have to check for the department-wise statistics for more accuracy of the data because some colleges are good at some branches only.

Once dream colleges are finalized, students must plan admission strategies. This involves adhering to admission timelines, preparing for entrance tests, gathering required documents, and planning interviews or discussions.

Make a list of 8 to 10 dream colleges for consideration:

1. ________________________________

2. ________________________________

3. ________________________________

4. ______________________________________

5. ______________________________________

6. ______________________________________

7. ______________________________________

8. ______________________________________

9. ______________________________________

10. _____________________________________

Chapter 14

STUDYING ABROAD

"Studying abroad is the single most effective way of changing the way we view the world."

– Chantal Mitchell

The idea of studying at Harvard or Oxford drives the dreams of millions of students from across the world. These Ivy League universities are often regarded as the best way to build connections worldwide and acquire a prestigious stature. Many students dream of studying abroad, drawn by the allure of these prestigious institutions and their promising career prospects.

This is not to say that studying abroad does guarantee success; however, it significantly boosts the odds. Students worldwide flock to popular study destinations like the USA, the UK, Australia, Canada, and Singapore every year.

However, before deciding and fixating on a particular destination, you should have answers to some critical questions:

- Which country would suit you best, including language, food, culture, etc.?

- Where are the best study and job opportunities for your particular stream of interest?
- What are the admission requirements?
- Which country is the most affordable?

Key criteria like reputation, job opportunities, education system, language requirements, entry ease, safety, lifestyle, and value for money will help choose the best study destination.

UNITED STATES OF AMERICA (USA)

The United States stands as the beacon of higher education, captivating students' imaginations worldwide, with a staggering 16% of international students choosing U.S. colleges and universities. Out of these 16%, most international students are from India. As a country that values education over everything else, Indian students are drawn to the promise of world-class education and diverse cultural experiences in these American colleges and universities.

This is not without reason. The USA has donned itself as an academic powerhouse, a lair for global connections, and has placed itself at the forefront of innovation in all sectors. This also correlates to the U.S.'s commitment to academia, the opportunity to diversify into different educational fields, and an immersive, hands-on training prospect. As such, international career counselors need to understand the intricacies of being a part of the U.S. academia and guide students who are seeking education in that foreign land.

Academic excellence in the USA owes widely to the large variety of courses they offer. The leading courses are the primary reasons that attract international talents, such as business management, engineering, liberal arts, medicine, and sciences.

The main intakes for universities in the U.S. take place during the Fall Semester (September/October), and the mid-year intake takes place in the Spring Semester (January/February). There are also summer intakes available for some universities, but not all international students can access them.

Education Costs in U.S. Universities

One of the most crucial factors when opting for an international university, especially a U.S. university, is understanding and analyzing the education costs. An international student might face higher tuition charges at state schools. At top-tier universities, mainly private, non-profit ones, the cost can be around $60,000 a year. However, there are other budget-friendly options, especially among public schools. You must consider that public universities often have different tuition rates for in-state and out-of-state students. Besides that, some community colleges offer two-year programs at lower costs, making them a great alternative. Also, scholarships and financial aid are some important points to factor in that immensely help in cost-cutting.

Regarding funding for education, the best option is to be prepared and look at all the varied options available at our behest. Notably, it's not the cost that differentiates between the quality of education one can receive.

Here are some smart strategies for choosing a university that won't drain your bank account:

- Choose public universities – they often have lower tuition fees.
- Choose universities in areas with a lower cost of living.
- Choose universities that offer significant need-based financial aid.
- Choose universities that provide scholarships for Indian and international students.
- Choose universities where you can shine academically.
- Go for a community college; they're a cost-effective option.

Understanding the education system is key to making the right choices for international students. The U.S. education system is more flexible, with a variety of options such as public and private universities, technical and vocational colleges, and community colleges to ensure that students can get a quality education at their own price.

Tests Required in the United States

With Indian students going to the U.S. increasing significantly by 30%, it is important to prepare with proper knowledge, especially for the entrance exams. These exams act as gatekeepers to your dream courses, so let's dive into the basics.

International English Language Testing System (IELTS):

When it comes to international tests, IELTS is the world's most important and widely recognized language proficiency test. The exam is designed to test English language skills for studying or working in the United States. The sections that make up this kind of test are listening, reading, writing, and speaking. It comprises two sub-tests: one is called Academic, and it is for people who want to pursue tertiary education or postgraduate studies, while the other one is General, which is suitable for people who wish to immigrate or attend training courses.

This examination allows candidates to appear in either online or offline mode. After about 13 days, the results are released and are valid for two years. These examinations are given scores on bands ranging from 1-9, with the majority of colleges admitting students with bands ranging between 7-9. More than 3,400 institutions in the USA accept these marks.

Test of English as a Foreign Language (TOEFL):

Another renowned English language test accepted by numerous institutions worldwide is the TOEFL test. The sections of this test are divided into reading, listening, speaking, and writing. It is meant to measure English proficiency in academic settings, with scores ranging from 0 to 120, with each section scored on a range of 0 to 30. For admission to universities, a good score is considered to be 100 out of 120.

Just like IELTS, this test score is also valid for two years. Students can sit for this test throughout the year, multiple times. The result of TOEFL is accepted by more than 8,500 colleges in over 130 countries, except for Canada and Australia.

American College Testing (ACT):

Conducted seven times a year, the ACT is a standardized test covering English, mathematics, Reading, and science subjects. Students of all grade levels can take this test, with scores ranging from 1 to 36. Both online registration and payment options are available for this test. The test scores are widely accepted by all four-year U.S. colleges and universities.

SAT Exam:

This is one of the most renowned American exams in the world, and students must have heard of it. This is an important test and is divided into SAT I (verbal and mathematical reasoning) and SAT II (subject-specific). It consists of reading, writing, math, and an optional essay section, with scores ranging from 400 to 1600. This test takes place five times a year and has flexible registration options with no limit on retaking the test.

The SAT II – Subject Tests are designed to measure knowledge and skills in specific subject areas and are an extra leverage when it comes to college admissions owing to their subject-specific method. There are 20 SAT Subject Tests in five general subject areas: english, history, languages, mathematics, and science. The test results for this, like others, are valid for two years.

Entrance tests are critical for U.S. admissions. As such, students are advised to start preparations early and take up coaching classes if needed. Registering early provides a good advantage, like providing additional time for test preparation. However, it is to be noted that U.S. universities evaluate students on factors that go beyond just test scores, making it essential to showcase your unique qualities.

UNITED KINGDOM (UK)

Another one of the world's top destinations for international students is the United Kingdom. The United Kingdom is one of Europe's most diverse countries, attracting a massive influx of international students each year. It's not an uncommon phenomenon to find Nobel Prize winners as alumni of several universities in the U.K. These universities are renowned for their globally recognized study programs and innovative research facilities that help students get the resources and help they need to succeed. Owing to their unique teaching approach, which emphasizes individual research as well as collaborative projects, students receive the best of critical thinking and practical skills to succeed in the job market.

What attracts international students to the UK is the presence of four of the world's top six universities, where students are guaranteed an advanced education and internationally recognized certifications. The name of any of these universities on their CV significantly increases their employment possibilities and gets them through most doors.

The universities present students with various study options to choose from, including short courses, certificates, diplomas, and undergraduate and postgraduate degrees. Similarly, students can access these courses through distance learning programs or by attending campus-based lessons. These flexible education modes have assisted learners coming from different backgrounds in getting a quality education regardless of their situations. In addition, it is important to note that UK institutions also offer highly competent staff as well as comprehensive support services.

When it comes to the financial strain, London has a high cost of living, making it the most expensive city, whereas universities in rural areas are more affordable. Meanwhile, schools have varying charges for tuition fees depending on the institution or subject chosen. Additionally, scholarships and financial aid opportunities may assist in such cases. The students who enroll in this program for at least six months get a chance to work for 20 hours weekly while they study, thus helping them significantly manage their cost of living, which includes, among others, housing, food, travel expenses, clothes, entertainment, and personal care.

In conclusion, therefore, the UK is considered one of the best places where you can get a world-class education in top universities with additional prospects to work with big companies, a support system in place, and excellent lecturers. All these are further sweetened by the presence of a multicultural society, vibrant cities, and rich cultural heritage that make someone coming from India feel right at home.

Tests Required for UK Universities

Just like in the U.S., students need to sit for some major tests to study in the U.K. Alongside the English proficiency tests like IELTS and TOEFL, students must also pass specific entrance exams for certain courses:

- **The Law National Aptitude Test (LNAT):** This is a 2-hour computer-based test consisting of two sections - multiple choice and an essay question. The results are directly forwarded to the applied university.
- **BioMedical Admissions Test (BMAT):** Divided into three sections, this is also a 2-hour test for medicine, veterinary, biomedical science, and dentistry applicants. The sections cover aptitude, scientific knowledge, and writing skills.
- **University Clinical Aptitude Test (UCAT):** This course is divided into five subtests to evaluate verbal reasoning, decision-making, quantitative reasoning, abstract reasoning, and situational judgment. This is required for admission into medicine and allied courses.

Method to Go Through the Application Process in UK Universities

Below are some of the steps students should take to apply for UK universities:

1. Register with UCAS or Universities and Colleges Admissions Service, fill out personal details, write a personal statement, and select up to five courses they want to apply.

2. Pay the application fee before obtaining a reference and submit your application online by the deadline.

3. For instance, an application process requires documents such as a valid passport containing IELTS scores [English language proficiency tests], a 10th marksheet/ grade card, a class 12 subject list, SOP [Statement of Purpose], and LORs [Letter of Recommendation].

4. The applied universities receive the applications via UCAS, after which it will take about 4-6 weeks for the results to be released. Such may include unconditional offers, conditional offers, or rejections.

However, prestigious universities like Cambridge, Oxford, and the London School of Economics & Political Science have entrance exams or preliminary online applications that add up to their admission procedures, apart from those highlighted above.

AUSTRALIA

Coming right after the UK and the US is Australia, which hosts the third-highest number of international students, offering over 22,000 courses across 1200 institutions. Anyone with a student visa can apply to any of the universities registered under the Commonwealth Register of Institutions and Courses for Overseas Students (CRICOS). CRICOS ensures the universities are on par with international student expectations. With this, students can apply to any of the 41 universities: 38 public and three private ones.

Education System:

- **Undergraduate:** Typically, three years (four for honours). It starts in February and July, with some institutions offering multiple intakes in September and November.
- **Postgraduate:** 1 to 2 years, typically starting in March, with variations by course and institution.
- **Doctoral:** 3 years, with flexible start dates that can be negotiated with supervisors. They also usually do not have any formal semesters.

The most popular courses in Australian universities include finance, Accounting, Hospitality, Education, Business Administration, Information Technology, and health.

Group of Eight (Go8):

These comprise Australia's top research universities and consistently rank among the world's top 100 universities. Notably, seven Go8 universities are in the top 100 globally, with all universities within the top 150 in rankings.

Entry Requirements:

- For undergraduate degrees, the IELTS score must be at least 6.5 with no section below six bands, and academic requirements are around 85% for most courses and 92-95% for medicine or nursing.

- The Group of Eight (Go8) universities do not accept the Indian state board curriculum.

Australia offers a platter of diverse courses, world-renowned universities, culture, and environment, all of which make it an attractive destination for international students.

SINGAPORE

Singapore is not only a great travel destination but a hub of premier education, with highly reputed institutions despite its small size. It is one of the most preferred educational destinations in the world, with over 80,000 students from 120 countries studying at Singapore universities. International students enjoy a massive advantage as Singapore offers a high standard of education at a lower cost compared to its Western counterparts.

Some of the most popular courses in Singapore include computer science/IT, Engineering, business, art and design, and social sciences.

Cost of Education:

The tuition fees at Singaporean universities can range anywhere from S$13,000 to S$35,000, with living expenses of approximately S$2,300 per month. Some of the government-funded institutions may also mandate international students to stay and work in Singapore for three years after graduation. It is to be noted that, unlike their Western counterparts, students cannot take up part-time work to fund their education and can only work after the completion of their undergraduate degrees.

Application Procedure & Timelines:

Students can apply online through the Office of Admissions website of their preferred university and upload the required documents, such as secondary and senior secondary mark sheets, IELTS/TOEFL scores, SAT scores, passports, certificates, proof of financial capability, and birth certificates.

Strategically located in the heart of Southeast Asia, Singapore is home to a multicultural environment where students from all over the world come together in harmony. It also provides a high standard of living and education at a more affordable cost compared to Western countries. Besides this, many global universities have established campuses and collaborations in Singapore, while their national universities also rank high worldwide. One of the most attractive factors is safety, with low crime rates and strict government regulations put in place to safeguard the interests of international students. All these make Singapore an ideal destination for international students.

HONG KONG

Over the years, Hong Kong has quickly climbed the ranks to become a prominent educational destination in Asia. With its proximity to India, accessibility, comparatively lower tuition costs, lower cost of living, and high education standards, it has become an ideal place for international students. The visa issues with Western nations have also made Hong Kong a more preferred option among Indian students.

Advantages:

- It has a lower tuition cost when compared to the USA or the UK.
- A gateway to mainland China, it offers a cosmopolitan lifestyle.
- It has a strong Indian community presence, making Indian students feel right at home.
- The university accommodation is cost-effective and of high quality.
- It also boasts a vibrant nightlife, nature treks, and accessibility to explore the rest of China.
- If students can become proficient in Mandarin, their job prospects in this leading financial hub can also improve.
- The most important factor is the availability of direct flights from major Indian cities.

Hong Kong has many world-class institutions, with almost 20 local degree-awarding institutions. It is well known for the world's best executive Business Management programs, and the universities also offer joint programmes in collaboration with prestigious global institutions.

Cost of Studying and Living:

The tuition fees in Hong Kong depend on the course and university selected by the student, with international tuition fees ranging from HK$100,000 to HK$265,000 per year. Another major cost for students is accommodation, which is approximately HK$15,000 to HK$45,000 per year for university-owned hostels or HK$96,000 to HK$180,000 for privately rented one-bedroom flats. Meanwhile, the additional living expenses are estimated at around HK$50,000 per year, depending on the student's lifestyle.

While more affordable than its Western counterparts, the costs might be an issue for some students. However, students here are exposed to quality education, cultural diversity, and accessibility. This makes it the perfect choice for international students looking for an enriching academic experience in Asia.

BASICS OF VISA PROCESS FOR U.S. AND U.K.

United States (U.S.)

In recent years, the visa procedure in the U.S. has become more stringent, and the demand has also significantly increased by almost 80%. Among the types of visas available, students must apply for the non-immigrant visa, especially the student visa or the F1 visa.

F1 Visa Process:

The F1 visa process is extremely time-consuming, making it important for students to start the process as soon as they receive their I-20 form. Here are the step-by-step procedures students must follow to get their F1 visa:

- **Obtain the i-20:** Universities issue an i-020 form or 'confirmation of acceptance of the student' as soon as a student gets accepted.
- **Pay the SEVIS Fee Online:** This is mandatory for all F1 visa applicants and can be paid through the SEVIS (i-901) system through a credit card. Once the amount is charged, the payment confirmation page must be saved and carried forward.
- **Complete the DS 160 Form Online:** This is submitted electronically to the Department of State website. The consular officer uses this to process visas and take a personal interview to determine student eligibility. Once done, you will receive an I.D. number and password to access the confirmation page.
- **Pay the Visa Fee:** An online fee payment must be paid through NEFT or offline at approved banks. After that, the students will receive a receipt number and then can schedule an appointment. Remember you are required to schedule two appointments.
- **Schedule Appointments:** The appointments need to be booked for the Visa Application Center (VAC) and the visa interview. Students must schedule the VACX appointment at least one day before the interview appointment date, which can be done online or through call centers. Once booked, students can see

the appointment letter, which must be attached to the interview.

- **Visit an Offsite Facilitation Center (OFC):** This is to submit biometric information, including fingerprints and photographs, at any OFC centre. These are only located in cities where the Embassy or consulate is located. It is required to make a prior appointment before visiting the OFC location.

- **Undertake the Embassy Interview:** Students must prepare for the interview, especially be clear about why they want to study in the USA and why they have picked the course and university they have applied to. They also must carry all important and relevant documents.

- **Wait for Visa Outcome:** The students will be informed of the decision the day they give their interview. If their visa is refused, their passport will be returned to them directly. If not, the passport will be returned with a visa stamp approximately one week after the interview.

Important Notes:

- Students cannot apply before three months of the start date – an important thing to remember.

- The student's personal bank account must consist of the minimum funds required for tuition and living expenses for 4-6 months, which can be around Rs. 30-35 lakhs, depending on the chosen university.

- For visa requirements to show eligibility, various financial sources are acceptable, including personal accounts, F.D.s, P.F., and LIC surrender value. However, business or corporate account funds are not permitted.
- It is advisable to pay 50% of the first-year fee before filing a visa to ensure that you are definitely going to the university. In case the visa is rejected, the amount is refunded by the university.
- For the visa interview, prepare for questions regarding colleges/universities, academics, finance, and plans for returning to India.
- Students must, without fail, arrive at the Embassy at least 30-45 minutes before the interview.
- It is important to note that visas cannot be filed without a Confirmation of Acceptance from the University.

United Kingdom (UK)

The visa process for the UK is fairly simple. Students need to apply for the Tier 4 (General) student visa, which is the only visa meant for full-time, long-term study in the UK.

Tier Four Visa Process

The procedure to apply for the visa includes the following steps:

- **Online Application:** Fill out the application form online from the country the student resides in.

- **Processing:** The application is processed through the nearest Visa Centre in the country they are applying to.

- **Interview:** A consular officer interviews applicants to determine visa eligibility, which lasts for approximately 3-5 minutes.

Important Financial Aspects:

- The minimum funds required for tuition, living, and miscellaneous expenses must be available in the student's bank account for 3-5 months before filing a visa.

- The acceptable financial sources include personal accounts, F.D.s, P.F., and LIC surrender value, while corporate accounts, shares, bonds, and gold loans are prohibited.

Additional Notes:

- For the application process, applicants must travel to the nearest Visa Centre.

- The interview questions asked in the visa office will cover college/university choices, academic plans, financial capacity, and intention to return to India.

- It is important to arrive 30-45 minutes prior to the scheduled interview.

While the visa process is intricate and time-consuming, what lies beyond it is an academic life that will help them flourish in their career. International destinations are life-changing, teaching students more than what the academic curriculum offers. If given the opportunity and the financial situation allows, students must explore the option of pursuing international education.

Note: The information given in this chapter is for basic understanding of the overseas education process. The admission process, costs, and visa processes may change from time to time. For the latest information for that particular year, one should visit the concerned websites or Overseas Educational Consultants.

Chapter 15

BEYOND ACADEMICS: BUILDING THE PERFECT PERSONAL PROFILE

"Begin somewhere. You cannot build a reputation on what you intend to do."

– Liz Smith

As per reports, 614 million students were enrolled in secondary education around the world in 2020. This number has drastically increased over the years. A significant number of these students aim to get into good universities, and many of them even aim to go to international colleges and Ivy League institutions. The competition is thus incomparable. As a result, universities today are looking for more than just academic qualifications and good marks. They are looking for profiles that stand out among the crowd and offer them a glimpse of an extraordinary student. These are students who are not only academically sound but are well-rounded individuals with certifications, extracurricular activities, hobbies, and a personality that can grab attention.

Universities are seeking these criteria as these very students will be the face of the college/university in the coming years. They judge students on the basis of their personal profile, making it an important factor for every student worldwide hoping to get into a leading university.

This chapter explores the type of profile building students must aim for, how the universities check for the perfect profile, and what it means to have a student resume. Let's begin.

Types of Profile Building

A perfect profile is one that exudes success, confidence, skill, and intelligence. These are certain aspects that can be a part of a student's profile. However, it is to be noted that not every student needs to check every box.

1. **Academic Excellence:** This is definitely a must-have criterion for a good profile. Good academic marks, a well-to-do score in standardized tests like SAT, ACT, GMAT, and GRE, language proficiency, and participation in academic competitions like the Olympiads are great plus points.

   Almost every student aiming for Ivy League universities fulfills this criterion, scoring at least over 95%, showing their mastery over the subject they are interested in. As such, this criterion is the most expected of the lot and, hence, is not a stand-out factor for a student applying to such a top-tier university.

2. **Extracurricular Activities:** Marks are not everything, and this point stands true in this segment as well. Universities put significant importance on

extracurricular activities like sports, drama, music, art, or community service. This points to a student's ability to look beyond academia and highlights their passion and interests.

It is to be noted that having a massive list of extracurricular activities is not the point. It is about showcasing progress in whichever activity the student decides to pursue. The emphasis is on quality rather than quantity.

For example, a student interested in basketball started as a novice player in the first year, then went on to lead the school team in the second year, won multiple awards, and moved to the state championship. This shows progression in the activity and is the accepted criteria rather than joining multiple sports and remaining a novice in each.

3. **Co-curricular Activities:** These include extra courses, summer classes, and specialization classes. These activities go alongside the students' academic curriculum and highlight their interest in their subject matter and beyond. A student's interest might be to hone their intelligence in diverse subject matters.

   For example, a student interested in computer science joining a creative writing course showcases a diverse set of interests and passions.

4. **An Avid Reader:** It is said 'if you cannot travel, read a book,' and rightly so. Books offer a plethora of

knowledge that goes beyond the academic syllabus. Universities do appreciate and consider this criterion in a student profile. It is a very underrated habit; however, it opens up multiple new horizons. Adding to that fact, there is no dearth of books in the world, and the genres are more than enough - fiction, non-fiction, books on art and culture, business and entrepreneurship, life skills, and fantasy.

5. **Entrepreneurial Spirit:** It is a great addition to a student profile. An entrepreneurial spirit points to a student's ability to hold a leadership position, their creative and innovative mind, and a will to aim for a bigger goal.

6. **Work Experience:** Herein, work experience refers to internships, part-time jobs, and remote or on-site real-world experiences that provide students with hands-on training. This showcases a student's capability and enthusiasm to go out into the world and challenge themselves in a setting that reflects the impact of their work. Additionally, it is a plus point when applying for a job.

7. **Personality Development:** Without a doubt, this is a very attractive feature for a university. Since universities have multiple criteria for admission, and one of them is an interview, having a great personality adds much-needed charm and charisma. Universities mostly prefer students with strong and confident personalities. A

personality is a reflection of a person and the abilities they possess other than the aforementioned criteria.

The focus here is on personality development objectives and areas of improvement for which there is no specific curriculum. It differs from person to person. Someone's area of improvement might be to be a confident speaker or debater. For someone else, it might be time management, creative skills, and so on.

8. **Personal Branding:** Branding is the word in today's world, and everyone is immediately attracted to anything that is a brand. Personal branding works in the same way. It makes the person an asset and a brand for the university as well, making this a sought-after aspect of a student's profile. It is recommended that students build a personal brand that pertains to their interest - it can be a blog, an Instagram page, a LinkedIn account, or a YouTube channel - whichever promotes them as a brand.

9. **Networking:** This is what I would call an extension of personal branding. Networking can take place through personal connections or through platforms like LinkedIn. Connecting with students, professors, or alumni from your dream university makes your personal brand more visible and familiar.

10. **Hobbies and Interests:** Last but not least, unique hobbies and interests are often seen as a personal aspect and not something to flaunt. However, when

it comes to a profile, a unique hobby or interest can make you stand out. You can be a storyteller, a weaver, a fashion blogger, a skater, or a graffiti artist - these are hobbies that immediately reveal more about the personality of a student. Hobbies and interests reveal more about the unique aspects they bring to the table.

How Are Universities Looking for The Perfect Profile?

Besides grades and tests, universities have come up with interesting and innovative methods to get to know a student beyond their academic pursuits, such as:

- **Video Essays:** This is the most interesting way of showcasing your profile. A video essay is like a traditional personal essay but with more technology and work put into it. Also, it is very exciting to work on and look at. The idea is to be as creative as possible.

- **Interviews:** Here is where, as previously mentioned, a student's personality shines. This is also the means through which universities get answers to their queries, like how well you know your subject matter. How interested are you in pursuing this course? What are your likes and dislikes? What are your interests and passions?

- **On-spot Essays:** It is quite nerve-racking, but it shows a lot to the university you are applying to. It showcases your creativity, quick thinking ability, writing and editing skills, knowledge about anything in the world, clarity of thought, and originality of ideas.

- **Aptitude Tests:** Universities use this to test a student's logical reasoning, verbal aptitude, quantitative aptitude, and data interpretation through a series of multiple-choice questions.

- **Portfolios:** This is a comprehensive method to display all that you have accomplished and pursued. A portfolio can be creative and intriguing, with links and certifications attached to it.

Ultimately, without a doubt, a strong profile or student resume is a must for college admissions. The perfect time for profile building is as early as the 9th grade, with plenty of time on their hands to hone their skills without the academic pressure of important exams. Students today need to go beyond the ordinary norms of good marks and look toward what truly defines them - their skills, passions, and interests.

Chapter 16

SETTING MILESTONES: ONE STEP AT A TIME

"I may not be able to live up to your expectations because I have set up my own milestones."

– Debasish Mridha

Life is a journey and not a destination. There is always the next step and the next goal to look forward to. Sometimes, it can get overwhelming, especially for students who have their entire life ahead of them. They are yet to graduate, give their first interview, crack their first job, earn their first salary, and so on. There is so much to do, and it might seem like everything is coming down simultaneously. Setting a milestone helps immensely in this scenario.

What Exactly are Milestones?

They are goals or checkpoints that you can set throughout your life. It maps where you have come from and where you must go next. It's like your life's travel itinerary but so much more impactful.

A person can have multiple significant milestones in their life, and for students, it marks their journey from studenthood to careerhood and what comes after that. Here, the question arises -

How to set a Milestone?

Regarding any milestone, the most common technique is the SMART framework - the smart way to set your goals. We have already explored this earlier, but let's do a quick overview from the milestone lens. The SMART framework has five steps or elements to it:

- **S – Specific:** Make your goal as specific as possible. This means not just saying, 'I want to complete this subject course,' but rather, 'I will complete Chapter 1 and Chapter 2.'
- **M – Measurable:** The idea of measuring your goals means you can track your progress more accurately. In this case, you can say, 'I will complete Chapter 1, pages 2-8, and Chapter 2, pages 8-12.'
- **A – Achievable:** Just setting a goal is not enough. It must be achievable by considering your resources, time, and ability to complete them. Making goals too difficult to achieve can make you lose confidence and focus. So if two chapters seem unachievable, set it as 'I want to complete Chapter 1, pages 2-8' instead.
- **R – Relevant:** If your goals are irrelevant to your bigger goals, it makes no sense to pursue them now. For example, you may have a science exam the next day, so studying for English is not relevant now.

T – Time-bound: Always, always set a timeline. It helps keep you on track, stops you from procrastinating, and keeps you accountable. In this case, you must set your goal as 'I will complete Chapter 1, pages 2-8 by 9 PM today.'

Besides this method, another goal-setting method is called the Tiered Goal Setting. The concept behind this is to divide your bigger goals into smaller and more manageable ones. To explain through an example, I have divided a career aspiration into 5-year, Annual, Quarterly, and Monthly goals-

1. **5-Year Goal:** Your 5-Year goal is the bigger destination. You have your timeline in place, but the goal itself is more complex and will take much time to reach. However, this goal helps you understand to what point and pace you need to progress.

2. **Annual Goal:** Setting a yearly goal, in this case, is to break down what you need to do annually to help you fulfill your bigger goal.

3. **Quarterly Goal:** This further breaks your annual goals into four quarters – Q1, Q2, Q3 and Q4. Most companies use this method to track employees' progress, and you can do that too for your personal goals.

4. **Monthly Goal:** This step helps you break down your quarterly goal into manageable sections of what needs to be done in months. Each month, you can have one goal that will take you close to your Q1 goal.

Your tiered goal-setting method does not have to stop here; you can go on to setting weekly and daily goals. You can also combine the Tiered and SMART goal-setting methods to keep you on track.

This might seem tedious and feel like too much planning, but it makes every goal seem more achievable since you know the steps to reach there.

It is to be noted that goals, once set, do not have to be written in stone. Your aspirations can change, and so can your steps to reach there. However, you should not change your goals because you feel lazy or are prone to procrastinating. Setting milestones depends massively on your willpower.

Student Goals Must-Haves

You must have or try to include some goals in your student life. According to research, there are five you might desire to have -

- **Career Counseling:** The important thing about having this as a milestone is to understand if you are walking the right path. A career counselor can guide you toward what you are good at and how to achieve it. It is especially a perfect milestone when you are confused about the course you must take or what career you are more inclined to pursue.
- **Academic Excellence:** Milestones for students must always include this step. A good career massively depends on the colleges and universities you get into,

for which marks are a prerequisite. However, it is not just marks; additional co-curricular activities are also a part of this process.

- **Extra-curricular Activities:** Besides academia, extra-curricular activities boost your student profile immensely. This must always be a point in your annual goal list.
- **Research Projects:** This is less talked about, but being part of research projects or prioritizing research helps you understand your career and goals more intricately. It can be research about anything you are interested in - it's a great tool to learn more about the world and everything in it.
- **Work Experience:** Internships and part-time work are all included in this section. As mentioned, work experience helps you get closer to your dream job.

Celebrate Your Milestones

No milestone is too small or insignificant to celebrate. Every small thing you do to reach your goals is a step toward the bigger goal, and if you did not do these small things, you could not have celebrated the big goal. As such, everything calls for a celebration.

It can be your graduation, your first interview call, your first job, your first resignation, retirement - every single thing. Some people would even tell you to celebrate your daily task completion.

Talking about tasks, a well-known method to help you concentrate is to follow the Pomodoro method, wherein you do your daily tasks in a 25-5 minute or 50-10 minute method (wherein the 25 and 50 minutes are the time you work, and the 5 and 10 minutes are for resting). For each completed concentration session, you treat yourself.

It cannot be emphasized enough how rewarding celebrating your tiniest goals helps keep you motivated and productive. Likewise, always walk a step at a time, i.e. concentrate on one goal at a time, which will keep you stress-free from the long list of tasks you might need to accomplish.

STEP III: WORLD OF WORK

The time has finally arrived to explore the much-awaited final section of the book 'The World of Work.' At this point, this section appears to be a prized possession. After toiling hard to understand oneself and going through the rigorous world of education, you finally have the first goal of your career—or rather, the beginning of your career that introduces you to the real world.

This is not to say that student life is not the real world; rather, the work life exposes you to unfamiliar situations, financial responsibility, and the feeling of being an adult who needs to make adult decisions.

Part III of the book will explore occupational theory, which reveals the complex world of professions and businesses, including our occupational choices and their impact on the workflow. It explores the job scene in the 21st century, where the typical nine-to-five has transformed into a flexible timeline, from full-time jobs to freelancing, from work-from-office to work-from-home culture.

This section goes on to explore the various new opportunities that have emerged in the professional world—one among many being entrepreneurship marked by innovation, risk-taking, and visionary leadership. We will also explore the career graph and how to climb the corporate ladder or move toward professional advancement. After all, the goal is to be the best at everything we aim for.

The section wouldn't be complete without 21st-century careers, which are laden with difficulties, and the emergence of technology, which has opened up more opportunities. We will also look into the gig economy, a decentralized marketplace with short-term contracts, freelance jobs, and on-demand services.

This final section will take you through the ups and downs of the real world of your career. With advice and suggestions, real-life anecdotes, and interesting examples, the aim is to provide a complete picture of the world of work.

Chapter 17

EXPLORING OCCUPATIONAL THEORY: FINDING YOUR PATH

"Find out what you like doing best and get someone to pay you for doing it."

– Katharine Whitehorn

Ever since childhood, you may have often been asked, "What do you want to be when you grow up?" You must have responded, "I want to be a doctor," "an astronaut," "a teacher," and "an engineer"—occupations that are well-known and those that you have grown up listening about. However, as you grow older, you realize that those are not the only types of occupations that exist in the world, and your childhood dream must have given way to adult decisions.

Before we move any further, it is important to understand what occupation means. Occupation is anything that keeps you occupied and something you spend a significant amount of time doing, either for pleasure or otherwise. This occupation earns you a livelihood, helps you live with dignity, and fulfills your financial obligations. Occupation is a person's principal activity that they do on a regular basis.

Types of Occupations

The International Standard Classification of Occupations (ISCO-08) divides jobs into ten major groups:

- **Managers**

  These people are in charge of organizations or divisions, determining objectives, making choices, and leading the work of others. They should have strong leadership skills as well as good communication and problem-solving talents. Individuals in this role include the COOs, the CEOs, the heads of departments, project managers, team leaders, and supervisors, as well as the operations and logistics managers.

- **Professionals**

  Such jobs require a lot of education and training, which sometimes includes a graduate degree or specialized certificate. They apply their knowledge to tackle complex problems and provide expert services. Professionals include doctors, lawyers, engineers, architects, scientists, researchers, academics, accountants, financial analysts, economists, teachers, professors, counselors, designers, authors, and artists.

- **Technicians and Associate Professionals**

  These positions stand between professionals on the one hand and non-professional workers on the other. They provide technical help or assist experts in performing their duties. They typically must have some postsecondary education or experience in a specified field. These professionals include nurses, dental hygienists, medical technicians, paralegals, legal assistants, engineering technicians, web developers, graphic designers, multimedia specialists, radiologists, and laboratory and environmental technicians.

- **Clerical Support Workers**

  This refers to a class of jobs offering support in administrative and record-keeping matters within the business. Job titles may include data entry, scheduling, communication, and other administrative duties. These workers include the receptionist, secretary, administrative assistant, customer service agents, call center agents, bookkeepers, accounting clerks, and data input & information processors.

- **Service and Sales Workers**

  These positions involve dealing with consumers to deliver services or sell products. They necessitate effective communication, interpersonal skills, and a customer service mindset. The workers include servers, bartenders, waitresses, chefs, hair stylists, barbers, cosmetologists, retail salespeople, cashiers, customer service representatives, travel agents, insurance agents, real estate agents, guards, personal care workers, and social service workers.

- **Skilled Agricultural, Forestry, and Fishery Workers**

  To work in natural resource industries, most occupations require specialized knowledge as well as abilities, as most of them frequently involve manual labor plus machine use, such as those of farmers, ranchers, agricultural laborers, fishermen, aquaculture workers, foresters, loggers, arborists, landscapers, and gardeners.

- **Craft and Related Trade Workers**

  These skilled workmen resort to their tools and hands to build, put in place, and fix structures and equipment. They are often hired for some particular undertaking or need a trade school or an apprenticeship program. A few instances of the same include plumbers, electricians, carpenters, mechanics, and others.

- **Plant and Machine Operators and Assemblers**

  These positions require operating machinery as well as equipment in factories or other places. Some on-the-job training may be required, but it is generally less than for a skilled trade. The people in this occupation include machine operators like CNC (Computer Numerical Control), milling machine operators, truck and bus drivers, and others.

- **Elementary Occupations**

  When entry-level jobs require little formal training with an emphasis on simple activities, they make up elementary occupations that can provide a good opportunity for obtaining work experience. A few examples of such jobs include janitors, cleaners, housekeepers, construction workers, manufacturing workers, agricultural laborers, and others.

- **Armed Forces Occupations**

  These people serve in the military, ensuring national security and conducting defense operations. They demand commitment, discipline, and physical fitness. Examples include Army, Navy, Air Force, Marine Corps, Coast Guard troops, officers, enlisted personnel and specialists, military pilots, mechanics, and intelligence experts.

The division of these groups does not stop here. They are further divided into sub-majors, minors, and units. These groups are divided based on their skill level and the amount of specialization required to acquire and hold these positions. The above-mentioned broader occupational groups have around 12,000 careers under them.

Three Sectors of the Indian Economy

The Indian economy, as of 2024, is the fifth-largest economy in the world and is rapidly growing. The contribution to these economies comes from three sectors of activity: extraction of raw materials (primary), manufacturing (secondary), and services (tertiary). Let's understand that in detail:

1. **Primary Sector**

   This sector occupies a 10% quota in the workforce. They are largely dependent on the availability of natural resources, as they are all connected with the extraction and production of the same. The occupations under this model include agriculture, fishing, mining, etc.

2. **Secondary Sector**

   This sector occupies 20% of the workforce and contributes almost 28% of the GDP. The products or services created in this sector depend on natural ingredients. The final product is meant for user consumption. As per value, this sector holds the best position. These are concerned with the processing of resources. The most common examples in this sector are the manufacturing and transportation industries.

3. **Tertiary Sector**

   This sector occupies 70% of the quota in the workforce and contributes the largest share of the GDP. This is the service sector, which provides support and advancement to the former two sectors. The industries under this include finance, IT services, consulting, and so on.

As per the concept of the model, an economy's main focus shifts from the primary to the secondary and finally to the tertiary as development takes place. Countries that have low per capita incomes and fall under the early stages of development derive most of their national income from production in the primary sector. The countries in the later stages of development that mainly have medium levels of national income draw most of their earnings from the secondary sector. Finally, the countries with high levels of national income, which are highly developed countries, depend mainly on the output of the tertiary sector. Understanding this model will help you unravel your nation's position in the economic fold.

Beyond Jobs: Understanding Careers and Professions

Now that you have a better idea of looking into specific jobs, let's differentiate between occupations, jobs, careers, and professions. While the various words are used synonymously with each other, they have their own distinct differences.

- **Occupation:** This is a broad term that is used to define a wide variety of roles with similar characteristics. Occupations can be a teacher, nurse, doctor, scientist, and other well-defined roles. These types of occupational roles offer security and longevity, and people can think of pursuing them as career options. However, in today's world, people change their occupational roles based on different circumstances.
- **Job:** A job is anything that pays the bills, meaning any work that you do in exchange for money. It can be short-term work, an odd job, contract work, or anything that is task-based. These may or may not be a long-term role.
- **Career:** This is a much broader topic and encompasses a person's entire life. This includes everything accomplished through their skills, experiences, and knowledge. A career is acquired over a long period of time, and it often showcases the trajectory of the

work you have done. This can be acquired by staying in the same field of work for a long time or even when a newer job role gets added to it.

- **Profession:** This requires formal training and education. A professional is someone who is skilled through rigorous training in a particular field and is often deemed an expert in the same. It can be a specialized doctor, a legal professional, and so on.

The occupational theory helps you understand the types of occupations that exist and where you might fit based on your interests and passion. Whether you want to be a follower, leader, innovator, or creator, there is a place for you. In today's century, there are more than enough career options to explore and fit your inkling. Furthermore, understanding how our choice of occupation impacts the economy is immensely motivating and helps us to put our best foot forward.

Chapter 18

EXPLORING THE WORLD OF JOBS

"Choose a job you love, and you will never have to work a day in your life."

– Confucius

As stated in the previous chapter, a job is anything that helps someone earn money. It can be a series of tasks or a limited set of functions, long-term or short-term. It can be any work for which an 'employer' pays a certain amount to ensure completion. It can be an odd job like mowing the lawn, or it can be used to define the work of a CEO. In other words, you have a job if you are occupied with a task that gets you money.

Broadly speaking, there are three types of jobs:

Instruction-based: A job where a person only needs to follow instructions and accomplish a task based on what they were asked to do. In such job roles, a supervisor assigns tasks and checks for completion. The workers are mostly paid by the hour. Retail salespeople, assembly line workers, and customer service personnel are a few examples of those who fall under this category.

Implementation-based: A certain level of supervision is provided in this type of job role. However, the majority of the task is to find the correct solution and implement it. This role mostly requires specialization and knowledge of the subject matter. Examples include nurses, electricians, and web developers.

Decision-based: This is a high-level job position and makes you the decision-maker. It requires a high level of understanding and experience in the subject, as well as the ability to make difficult choices. This position holds the maximum amount of responsibility. Examples include doctors, attorneys, and CEOs.

Types of Jobs: By the Collar

The concept of unofficially denoting job roles through the color of a person's collar worn at work began during the late 20th and 21st centuries. They were often metaphorical or stereotypical descriptions of job roles depending on the type of work done, skills, work environment, and so on. These collar definitions were often associated with pay, social class, and even outdated gender norms. The most famous collar jobs, since the earliest times, were white and blue-collared jobs. However, over the years, many other collar jobs have emerged. Let's explore them in brief:

- **White Collar**

  This mainly denoted salaried professionals who worked in an office setting. They often held clerical, administrative, and managerial positions. Many jobs that require a shirt and tie are actually low-paying and high-stress, especially in the modern service and technology sectors. White-collar workers are known as suit-and-tie workers who work in service industries and often avoid physical labor.

- **Blue Collar**

  They were manual laborers who earned an hourly wage based on the amount of work done. Examples include people working in manufacturing, warehousing, mining, excavation, electricity generation, power plant operations, and so on.

- **Pink Collar**

  This collar denotes the people who work in the service industry and hold positions like waiters, retail clerks, salespersons, certain unlicensed assistive personnel, and others. They are mainly part of the working class and were often stereotyped as women-held job roles. The definition has been redefined to encompass other roles as well.

- **Gold Collar**

  This worker is a highly skilled multi-disciplinarian or knowledge worker who combines intellectual labor—which is typically white-collar—with the manual labor of blue-collar positions. They usually engage in problem-solving or complex technical work in fields such as academic/scientific research, engineering technicians, and advanced technology industries.

Besides these, there are a few newer collar roles, like

- **New Collar:** Someone who acquired technical and soft skills through a non-traditional educational path.
- **No Collar:** A free-spirited worker often denotes artists who prefer to follow their passion rather than the money that comes with it.
- **Green Collar:** Refers to people who work with the environment and renewable energy, but also refers to military personnel.
- **Open Collar:** The new-age worker who works from home via the Internet, like a freelancer.
- **Grey Collar:** Often used to define elderly individuals working beyond the age of retirement, as well as those occupations with elements of both blue and white collar.

Find the Right Job

Having a job that pays for your lifestyle is important; however, what is more important is finding a job that makes you happy. Now that you know about occupation and the different types of job roles available in the market, it is time to go within and look at your passion and interests.

An ideal job gives you internal satisfaction, pays you a sustainable amount, utilizes your skills, and is something you are enthusiastic about. Your ideal job may not be the same as someone else's, which does not diminish its value or position in society.

Job satisfaction, in today's time, is the goal of any type of work. It reflects a person's happiness and level of satisfaction while working in their job role. If a certain role is not giving you internal peace, it's time for a break or a search for a different role. The world of work is constantly evolving, and hence, individuals must also be in the space of growing with the industry.

Chapter 19

THE PROFESSIONAL FIELD

"Let passion drive your profession."

– Oprah Winfrey

In Chapter 17, we explored a short snippet of what a profession means. To reiterate once again, a profession is a paid occupation that requires formal training and education. A person referred to as a professional is skilled through rigorous training in a particular field and is often deemed an expert in the same. It can be a specialized doctor, a legal professional, and more.

Before we dive into the intricacies of the profession and what it entails, let's take a quick history tour to understand its importance.

The profession has always been grounded in specialized educational training, where professionals impart their objective views on a subject solely for the benefit or use of others. During medieval times, only three professions were recognized: divinity, medicine, and law. The people who practiced them were regarded as learned professionals. They were regarded as highly valuable members of society for their understanding and expertise in their subject matter. Cut to today's time, and the importance provided to these three professions remains to this day—religious leaders like priests, doctors, and lawyers still hold a high-value position in society. These are also some of the most sought-after professions in the world, even today.

It must, however, be noted that while the prestige of a profession might not diminish over time, its status and power go through changes, especially when it comes to monetary compensation. People in the same profession often don't get paid the same way. To state an example, the salary earned by a doctor and a nurse, who both work in medicine, varies significantly.

Over the years, several other disciplines have been formalized and have acquired the status of a profession owing to the intricate nature of these disciplines and the need for formal education to manage them. Among the list of modern professions, surveying or land surveying achieved the status of a profession first, and then it also started to include others like dentistry, civil engineering, logistics, architecture, and accounting. With the advent of technology and occupational specialization, other disciplines like mechanical engineering, pharmacy, veterinary medicine, psychology, nursing, teaching, librarianship, optometry, and social work received the 'profession' status by the 1900s.

The journey of these disciplines turning from occupation to profession was marked with some significant milestones like becoming a full-time occupation, establishing a training school, a university school, a local association, a national association of professional ethics, and state licensing laws.

Once any occupation could check these milestones, they received the prestigious position of a 'profession'.

We can thus understand how much importance a profession holds, not only in terms of livelihood but also in how society perceives an individual. Today, thanks to the formalization of numerous occupations, individuals have a wide category of professions to choose from.

Types of Professions

1. **Corporate or Business Professionals:** They are individuals who hold managerial and technical positions in large corporations. Roles include product managers, HRs, analysts, salespersons, supervisors, and so on.

2. **Science and Engineering Professionals:** They hold a wide variety of roles across fields that require specific scientific knowledge or engineering expertise. Roles include geographer, researcher, astronomer, computer scientist, and so on.

3. **Information Technology:** This is the most booming sector in today's time and includes job roles like data scientist, technical writer, DevOps engineer, AI engineer, and more.

4. **Service Professionals:** For small and family businesses, the Service industry is the perfect ground for advancement. This industry has always been a necessity in society and, in today's time, is gaining

more prominence. Roles include baker, bartender, chef, customer service, tutor, fitness trainer, and so on.

5. **Creative Professionals:** The creative industry is the most competitive of the lot and the most sought-after. Since people's tastes and perspectives change constantly, so does the difficulty level for a creative professional. Roles include actor, journalist, photographer, writer, designer, and more.
6. **Professional services:** These include all the professionals who earn value through the knowledge of their work, which sometimes may not be acquired through formal education. They are the people who understand the best way to get a particular work done and offer their services to others at a price. Roles include gardener, architect, financial planner, apprentice, etc.
7. **Construction and Trades Professionals:** These professionals are experts in building, installing, maintaining, and repairing things. Roles include blacksmiths, technicians, laborers, electricians, equipment operators, and more.
8. **Government and Institutional Professionals:** These are professionals employed by the government or major institutions like universities and hospitals. Roles include politicians, firefighters, military personnel, teachers, paramedics, sociologists, social workers, and more.

Why is it Important to Choose the Right Profession?

Choosing a profession is a job in itself and needs immense scrutiny. We have already explored in previous chapters how to select a stream of work that suits your personality and needs. It involves taking personality tests to understand your interests, doing in-depth research to understand how different professions work and what suits your career growth, and attending career counseling that can help you receive the expert guidance you will need.

Thus, it is now necessary to focus on why choosing the right profession is so essential:

1. **A Lifelong Commitment:** An individual spends the majority of their life working, which includes 40+ hours per week. Doing something that you may absolutely hate for your entire life will leave you unsatisfied, stressed out, and unfulfilled in your career. It is, thus, important to choose a profession that aligns with your passions and makes you feel good. The right profession is one that you feel excited about every day and makes you feel energized.

2. **Financial Security:** Your profession is your means to financial fulfillment, so proper research and choosing the right one means you don't have to feel financially drained. In addition, doing something you love means being great at it, which equals bigger promotions and higher jumps in the financial scale.

3. **Continuous Learning:** Being professional means there is always the premise of learning constantly and growing constantly as the scope of your field expands. A professional must always aim to upskill themselves, which makes considering this point very important.

4. **Giving Back to Society:** Being a professional comes with a network of professionals in your field and adjacent fields. It is like your community that helps you thrive and progress in your career. It also promotes the idea of altruism and motivates you to do good for society. A profession isn't only meant for personal gain but rather to use your extensive knowledge to help those who don't have it.

Choosing a profession that supports your aspirations and interests is paramount for students or individuals of any age. The foremost concept is to pursue something you love and enjoy, and the rest is bound to fall in line.

Chapter 20

THE INS AND OUTS OF ENTREPRENEURSHIP

"The hardest part about being an entrepreneur is that you'll fail ten times for every success."

– Adam Horwitz

Being an entrepreneur might not be the easiest choice to make. However, when done right, it is the most rewarding. Entrepreneurs are individuals who have the passion and the interest to ideate, innovate, establish, and scale a business through massive risks and enjoy the majority of the profit. These individuals are often visionaries who strive to fulfill their dreams, following unconventional career paths filled with challenges but determined enough to accomplish them.

Entrepreneurship is an essential component of the global economy. It contributes to the local economy, provides job opportunities, and helps other businesses thrive.

Types of Entrepreneurship

If you're interested in starting your own business, it's first important to understand the types of entrepreneurship that exist and the one that most suits your interest.

Entrepreneurship is classified into four categories-

1. **Small Business Entrepreneurship**

   These can be regarded as local entrepreneurship or businesses. They consist of hairdressers, shop owners, plumbers, carpenters, and so on. These entrepreneurs do not plan to scale big and earn millions in revenue. Their sole motivation is to fulfill the financial needs of their family. They often hire their own family members or local employees to run their business.

2. **Startup Entrepreneurship**

   This type of entrepreneurship has seen a steep rise in recent years and has been very successful in its ventures, too. Startup entrepreneurs are often innovators who venture into entrepreneurship to change the world with their creations. They are also problem solvers, attract investors who think the same as them, and hire creative and innovative minds who can think out of the box. These startups need the most venture capital to start and sustain their business idea.

3. **Large Company Entrepreneurship**

   This entrepreneurial venture has a complete life cycle planned out. They offer the most job opportunities and are dedicated to staying in the market for the longest time. They constantly bring new, innovative products into the market connected to their primary product. These innovations are either self-created or bought to sustain their brand in the competitive business space. With the change in customer preference and business landscape, the product range also goes through major adaptation.

4. **Social Entrepreneurship**

   The sole goal of this type of entrepreneurship is to work for society and do good for them. They focus on creating products and services for the social good without concentrating on financial gain.

How to Become an Entrepreneur?

The idea of becoming an entrepreneur and running your own business might be very intriguing, and rightfully so. Most entrepreneurs are driven by the passion to bring their ideas to life or to solve a problem that could earn them millions. While others enjoy the freedom of being their own boss and the responsibility of providing employment to others. To be an entrepreneur, there are specific steps you must consider-

1. **A Business Plan:** Just wanting to be an entrepreneur is not enough. You must have an idea that would fuel your business. You must be able to answer these questions - What does your target audience need? Are you solving a problem through your idea? Are you creating a product that will revolutionize the market? Is your idea novel? How will you gather the funds to start and sustain the business? On top of these questions comes the most important one – are you

passionate about this venture, and does it align with your interest?

2. **Funds:** The most important aspect is to not only start your entrepreneurial journey but also to sustain it. You need the source and the ability to collect funds to fuel your business. Some entrepreneurs use their personal funds to start their ventures, while others look for like-minded investors or collect funds through crowdfunding. There are others who pursue venture capital and even those who look into business loans. Depending on your financial capability and understanding of your business, the financial options need to be sorted on priority.

3. **Resources:** This depends on your business model. You may need to source inventory, secure a lease, hire staff, or develop a shipping strategy. Your business plan must take each of these things into account. No two businesses are entirely alike; as such, their resource requirements also vary.

4. **Brand Strategy:** After you have the backend of your business sorted, it is time to establish a brand identity – how will people look at your company? A suitable logo, brand concept, dedicated website or application, and marketing strategy must be in place. Once done, you're ready to launch your business and proclaim it to the world.

5. **The Will to Learn:** Even if you are a product of business school or have gone through entrepreneurial training

> or courses, the business world is unpredictable. There is a lot to learn in the field, and you must be open to the idea of gathering knowledge. You must also be open to the idea of failing and learning from your mistakes. Most successful business ventures are built on the concept of doing their best despite all adversity and being humble enough to learn repeatedly until you get it perfect.

In the evolving business landscape, individuals, especially students, must set high goals and look at their careers from an entrepreneurial lens as well. The world is rapidly changing, and as such, entrepreneurship has a vast scope. Besides the risks associated with it, it also brings in mighty rewards for those smart enough to traverse this path with knowledge and skill.

Chapter 21

TRAVERSE THE LAND OF CAREER HIERARCHY & PLANNING

"The best way to predict the future is to create it."

– Abraham Lincoln

You might assume that planning for your career ends with getting your first job and that it is the gradual, expected climb from there on. However, the reality might end up surprising you. Climbing the corporate ladder is a process that requires careful planning. It is also linked to your own personal satisfaction. You might enjoy the comfort of being steady at a job for the time being but will slowly lose interest in your job when the work seems too monotonous, or it doesn't challenge you enough. It is, thus, important to not only plan out your career from the get-go but also understand the graph you want to climb.

Career Hierarchy

A corporate career hierarchy looks something like this:

1. **Entry Level:**

   Almost every individual starts from this position – whether a newly graduated or someone changing industries. This position mostly has the lowest salary, but it is a great place to learn and gather industry experience.

2. **Intermediate or Experienced (Senior Staff)**

   They do not hold any supervisory role in this position; however, they must have experience or specialized education in the industry in which they work. The individuals in this role often require less supervision and are often given the opportunity to work independently and take charge of projects.

3. **First-level Management**

   The individuals in this position ensure that the functions of a company are running smoothly. This position comes with supervisory duties, with the entry-level and intermediate positions reporting to them. These individuals come with both experience and qualifications and are often the point of contact for most employees in the company.

4. **Middle Management**

   They are the middlemen between the first-level management and the executive management. They report to senior management, who do not personally oversee the work of the different departments. They often act as advisers to the senior management and have teams working under them.

5. **Executive or Senior Management**

   They are also regarded as holding the 'C-level' or 'C-suite' positions like CEO, CFO, and so on. They are the heads of the company and oversee the financial well-being, the vision and mission, and the growth graph of the organization. These individuals come with years of experience or specialization in a particular field. They either climb the ranks in their organization or are hired from outside. They are also the ones with the highest package in the company.

Everyone in the corporate sector must always aim for the highest level, and your career planning must be able to determine how to get there.

Maslow's Hierarchy of Needs

Abraham Maslow, an American psychologist, had mapped out a hierarchy of needs and a theory of motivation that lets a person plan out their career based on their position at that time. He has listed out five steps to this hierarchy, which stem from the Theory of Motivation, which states

1. A person acts to satisfy their unmet needs.
2. There is a hierarchy of needs.
3. Once a need is met, we grow unsatisfied again and need to move to the next higher level to satisfy the new set of unmet needs

He has connected this idea to Maslow's Hierarchy of Needs, which goes like this -

1. **Physiological Needs**

   This is the most basic of the job roles and fulfills our basic needs like food, shelter, water, and so on. In this position, the central goal is to earn a livelihood to survive. People in this need level go for part-time, minimum wage, and on-call job roles.

2. **Safety Needs**

   Now that the primary need is fulfilled, the person seeks a full-time job that offers stability and security. They also look for additional perks like health insurance and the ability to go beyond basic needs and look for luxury. This is also when individuals look for their dream place or company to work at.

3. **Love and Belonging**

   This need level stems from a human's nature as a social animal. Now that their basic and safety needs are met, they look for long-term connections and networks in personal and professional relationships. They build networks to climb up in their careers and to open a gateway to learn from others.

4. **Esteem**

   The need here is to earn the respect, recognition, status, and prestigious position that comes from holding a senior position in a reputable organization. People who have fulfilled all the other aforementioned needs go forward to accomplish this need.

5. **Self-actualization**

   Once the esteem or the recognition has been achieved, and people go for higher goals that might transcend the organizational structure. They might wish to become their highest self, i.e., the highest position in a company, or start something that puts them at a higher level. The self-actualization stage is to realize one's full potential.

Everyone goes through these five hierarchies of needs, albeit their pace may differ from one another. Some others may skip one level altogether if it is already met through other means. For example, someone might not go through the physiological needs phase at all since it is already met, probably through the safety net provided by their parents' earnings. They aim for higher goals once they have accomplished one need and feel dissatisfied with remaining at the same level. It is to be noted that it's easier to move faster at the initial level, but as we climb through the needs, it takes more time and effort. This is because the higher level comes with more responsibility, and individuals need to uphold a higher standard of expertise.

Chapter 22

BE A PART OF THE GIG ECONOMY

"Now we have a gig economy where many people are holding down several jobs at once. The whole concept of a 40-hour week makes people under 30 laugh."

– Katrina Onstad

Since the COVID-19 pandemic disoriented the world as we once knew, and with the advancement of technology, how people approach work has massively changed. The 9-5, 40-hour work week is no longer the only norm. The work market has drastically been altered in recent years. It has given a stable and rapid rise to the gig economy.

The gig economy consists of independent workers, part-timers, freelancers, and contract workers who work gigs or temporary, time-bound jobs to earn a livelihood. Over the years, many gig platforms have sprung up, like Uber, Doordash, Blinkit, Upwork, and so on. These companies offer the workers the opportunity to work at their own time and at their own pace.

If you're a student who has recently graduated and does not want to climb the corporate ladder, you can consider this role. Or if you're an experienced employee wanting more flexibility in your life, this might be a good thing to step into. After all, the gig economy offers a lot of benefits.

For one, it offers flexibility. You are not answerable to anyone apart from yourself. You work at your own timeline and at your own pace. You take up projects that align with your interests at a price point you negotiate with your client. When you work and how long you work is up to you. You are your timekeeper, your own boss, your own agent.

The role does offer a tremendous amount of independence. As the sole decision-maker, you can determine the best way to tackle a job. You do not need to follow anyone's direction if you do not want to. In addition, you also save a lot of money by staying at home or working remotely and a lot of time by cutting down on travel hours.

However, it is not all rainbows. It also comes with some disadvantages. The responsibility of searching for your gigs is on you. Most people do not immediately get projects when they start offering services, often leading to unwarranted stress. The monetary aspect is also a thing to consider. There is no steady income, and gig workers are paid per gig. Some months are better than others.

Working alone often brings about loneliness, and workers usually feel like they are losing motivation to push themselves to work. Thankfully, all these have a solution that requires gig workers to put their best foot forward at all times.

How to be a Successful Gig Worker?

You have already understood the advantages and disadvantages of the gig economy. If you are inclined to go through this non-traditional career route, you can always use some tips on how to make it work.

1. **Build a Portfolio**

   The basis of gig work is to have a portfolio that showcases all the work you have accomplished, the skill sets you possess, and the industries you are in. A portfolio is an excellent way for clients to understand if you're the perfect fit for their requirements. It is also the ideal way to systematize your work and see the growth you have achieved over the years.

2. **Network**

   The next step is to build connections and network with people as much as you can. You must be active on job portals and gig sites to not only network with potential clients but also to ensure you can be one of the first to throw your hat in the ring. This also helps reduce your loneliness by having like-minded individuals and other gig workers in your network with whom you can connect for suggestions and queries.

3. **Promote Your Services**

   It's a section of networking, and it is equally important, if not more. You must actively promote your services and build yourself as a brand. Especially if your services are in the creative or intellectual section. For example, if you're a writer, you must promote yourself as a good writer by showcasing the projects you have completed, testimonials from your clients, and even sharing educational content to show yourself as an expert in your field.

4. **Set Your Prices**

   The best thing about being a gig worker is the ability to set your own price points for your services. You must understand the market and place a fair price on the amount of work you have to do for a particular project. Whether you get paid by the hour or otherwise, you must always set a rate that justifies your work.

5. **Get Your Act Together**

   This just means you must have a routine and a set place to keep you motivated and in high spirits for work. Even though you have the flexibility of time, workers have found that having a routine and a dedicated workspace greatly helps them concentrate and produce the best work. It also helps maintain a healthy schedule in the midst of handling it all.

A significant population today is part of the gig economy, whether through a secondary means of income or as full-time gig workers. It has also transformed the way companies work and hire talent. Since companies save a lot of money while getting the best workers for their projects, they often prefer this option. The gig economy, as such, might be the future norm of the working industry.

Chapter 23

NAVIGATING THE 21ST CENTURY CAREERS

"The illiterate of the 21st century will not be those who cannot read and write, but those who cannot learn, unlearn, and relearn."

– Alvin Toffler

The world of work is no longer the way it used to be. It is no longer the century of 9-5 or holding down a stable job until retirement. This is no longer the age where one job sustains a livelihood, or just having a few skill sets can help you scale your career. Not to scare you, but the way we view careers has drastically changed with technological growth and economic upheaval. Unfortunately, the current educational institutions and system have not been able to keep up with this rapid, monumental change. Thus, it falls on the students, the guides, and the parents to craft a career path that aligns with 21st-century careers.

In recent years, you must have noticed several new job roles like UI/UX designers, data scientists, social media managers, SEO specialists, and so on. Less than a decade ago, you might not have even thought of the job roles that exist on such a massive scale today. The future century also holds several other careers and professions that haven't been considered yet. And with that, several of the existing roles will disappear. Experts already predict that the 4th industrial revolution will take away millions of jobs thanks to automation. Still, it will also create millions of others in the fields of mathematics, computer science, architecture, and engineering.

Skills for the 21st Century Careers

The 21st Century Careers come with a list of skills that are highly advanced in nature. The population worldwide is more educated than ever before, bringing in more competition in every space. Individuals, thus, cannot be good at only one thing and expect to lead the line. They need to expand their skills and adapt to the changing times.

- **Essential Skills:** Basic skills have evolved drastically, and advanced reading, writing, and computational skills are now a must-have. These are the skills that have become a necessity in all kinds of jobs. Reading helps with studying graphs and technical documents, and writing ensures good communication skills. With technological advancements, to possess computational skills is a given.
- **Technical Skills:** This refers to the computer skills individuals in the 21st Century must possess. Everything today is online, and a variety of advanced information, telecommunications, and manufacturing technologies are being used in the job market every day. The ability to use IT for more productive and efficient work is a major skill set.

- **Organizational Skills:** Today's professionals must have the necessary problem-solving, analytical, creative, communication, and interpersonal skills to advance in their careers. This is no longer the requirement for only managerial positions. Even employees in non-managerial positions have to be a part of daily meetings and presentations that require them to utilize these skills.

- **Company-specific Skills:** The competitive world has forced companies to constantly bring in new, innovative products and services that help them retain their position. With the constant market change and technological upgradation, companies need to focus on continuous improvement. As such, employees must upgrade their skills and knowledge to stay relevant to the company's requirements.

This changing trend raises the question of what 21st century career options look like. While there are new emerging career options that are still unheard of today, like job developer, space mechanic, robot technician, image consultant, retirement counselor, and more, as per reports, some have retained their pace and will continue to do so. These include:

- **Healthcare sector:** Administration, Nursing, Physical health, Dentistry, Mental health

- **Technology sector:** Biotechnology, Engineering, Information Technology

- **Business and Professional Services:** Financial Services, Human Resources, Law, Communications, Public Relations, Sales and Marketing
- **Public Service:** Social Services, Education, State and Local Government

Besides these, if you are looking for high-paying jobs in the 21st Century, there are a few prominent ones like Web Developer, Video Game Designer, Application Developer, Registered Nurse, Physical Therapist, Data Scientist, Software Engineer, and more.

While the 21st century careers are going through rapid change and will continue to evolve, what will keep aspiring professionals in the game is their ability and will to upgrade themselves. It is also beneficial to keep an eye on the changing trends to ensure you are not missing out on the bigger, emerging opportunities in the market.

MY CAREER CLARITY BLUE PRINT

(To fill in your choices, use the extract of each relevant chapter)

Sl. No.	Element	Write your Choice
1.	My Calling	
2.	My Vision	
3.	My Mission	
4.	My Goals	Personal: Professional: Financial:
5.	My Values	
6.	My Personality	
7.	My Interest/Passion	
8.	My Aptitude and Intelligence	
9.	My Learning Style	
10.	My 21st Century Skills (Life Skills)	
11.	My Career Options	

Sl. No.	Element	Write your Choice
12.	My Course Options	
13.	My College Options	
14.	My Country Options	
15.	My Profile Building Activities	
16.	My Milestones (year-wise)	
17.	My Dream Occupations	Job: Profession: Business:
18.	My Dream Company	
19.	Career Milestones	1-5 Years: 5-10 Years: 10-20 Years: 20-30 Years:

This is the Career Clarity Blueprint which will act as a guide and self-realization piece of paper throughout your career. Take a printout and fill this at every milestone.

THE NEXT ACTION PLAN

The chapter marks the conclusion of the book. From the onset, you have discovered yourselves, your calling, vision, mission, goals, and values. You have uncovered your personality, interests and passions, aptitude and multiple intelligence, your personal learning style, and the 21st century skills that are required and that you possess today.

Once you are done exploring your inner self, you have stepped into the career pathway, which has given you a detailed understanding of the types of careers, the courses you must undertake for them, the colleges you can attend, and the countries you can target for education abroad. You have also learned the importance of building a profile and setting milestones throughout your career.

And finally, you have entered adulthood into the world of work, where you have learned about occupational theory and navigated the world of jobs, professions, entrepreneurship, and the gig economy. You have also received a peek into career planning and what the future of the 21st-century career looks like.

It has been quite a long journey and a roller-coaster at that. With this, you have taken part in building your career from scratch, in theory at the least. It is now time to put all this knowledge into practical use and start with your personal career journey. The Career Clarity Blueprint is always there to guide you along the way.

www.ingramcontent.com/pod-product-compliance
Lightning Source LLC
LaVergne TN
LVHW041026150826
845672LV00001B/222

* 9 7 9 8 8 9 5 5 6 0 4 7 1 *